Halloween
Collectible Decorations
and Games

Pamela E. Apkarian-Russell
Photography by Christopher J. Russell

394.2646 Apkarian c.1
Apkarian-Russell, Pamela.
Halloween collectible
decorations and games /

4880 Lower Valley Road, Atglen, PA 19310 USA

Designed by "Sue"
Type set in Americana XBd BTheading font/ text font Humanist 521 BT

ISBN: 0-7643-1027-5
Printed in China
1 2 3 4

Published by Schiffer Publishing Ltd.
4880 Lower Valley Road
Atglen, PA 19310
Phone: (610) 593-1777; Fax: (610) 593-2002
E-mail: Schifferbk@aol.com
Please visit our web site catalog at
www.schifferbooks.com or write for a free catalog.
This book may be purchased from the publisher.
Please include $3.95 for shipping.

In Europe, Schiffer books are distributed by
Bushwood Books
6 Marksbury Ave.
Kew Gardens
Surrey TW9 4JF England
Phone: 44 (0)208 392-8585
Fax: 44 (0)208 392-9876
E-mail: Bushwd@aol.com
Free postage in the UK. Europe: air mail at cost

Please try your bookstore first.

We are interested in hearing from authors
with book ideas on related subjects.

Contents

Acknowledgments

How does one thank all the hundreds of people who, over the years, have shared my Halloweens—which last for 365 days a year? How can I thank family, friends, and complete strangers who have encouraged me and added to my collection? How much richer I am for the stories and the memories of so many people who have shared their Halloweens-past with me. How fortunate I am that so many people have shared their information with me or have let me know that certain items were lurking out there, waiting for me. How often have people given me items that they thought should be in my collection? I don't know, but over the past thirty years I am sure it has been many. Every item, no matter, how mundane in their estimation, has been kept and cherished! Okay, so I ate the cookies out of the box ... or we had the cereal for breakfast ... or the article of clothing has been worn to the point that some of the mannequins don't even want to wear them, but the boxes or packaging or articles are kept and cherished!!

To all of you who didn't laugh but enjoyed my enjoyment and encouraged me, thank you, as you made this book possible. Anyone with a hefty check book can amass a collection, even with today's inflated prices; but, few are as fortunate as I, who can point with pride to items that have the provenience of good will and friend-ship, spanning such a long period of time. I have been blessed and I wish you all to know, even though I have not been able to thank you individually here, that you have made each of my books possible and have brought light and brightness to my life. Thank you from the bottom of my pumpkin-shaped heart!

A special thank you goes to the following people: Kathy Bowen, Rebecca Venable, Susan Erickson, Andy Brown of the Gotham Book Mart, Linda Witherill, Edward Gory, Ben Swanson of the American Dental Museum, and, above all, Elayne Star. If I have forgotten anyone, I'm sorry! If an item has appeared in the book and was a gift and I didn't acknowledge you, do let me know. The years speed by like a howling gale and my memory is like a candle in a jack-o'-lantern...it flickers and sometime goes out.

Like the vivid colors of the maple trees in autumn, life is short and fragile. From the bud in the springtime to the floating, falling leaf born up by the wind in the autumn, we can only be kissed by the sun and caressed by the rain if fortune smiles on us. If she does not, we are scorched, parched, or drowned. Dame Fortune has been very kind as my friends have been many and true and my family supportive. I thank them for their acceptance of my passion. Thank you, also, to all the Trick or Treat Trader subscribers who have encouraged me, kept me informed and stimulated me.

To all of you, Blessings! May your every day be full of happiness. Happy Halloween!

This is a very unusual Southern folk art piece by Flowers. It is not only a jug but a hanging wall sconce! The tongue has a red glaze on it, and it is so Krampus like! Krampus or Grampus is the hairy devil like creature who, in Austria, goes around with Santa Claus and beats up the bad people. He has a long tongue and carries a switch. He is scary and the celebrations in Austria are, I understand, rather hairy! $250

Introduction

It's dark out there, and the wind is blowing. The moon is full and I can see a dragon walking on the street below. A gaggle of witches, giggling and gawking at a group of pirates and G.I. Joes, are coming up the stairs. The candles are flickering in the grinning, toothsome jack-o'-lanterns and I'm scared... Hold my hand, it's shaking, and I don't want to drop my candy on the ground. Happy Halloween.

There is nothing quite so romantic and exciting, exhilarating and scary, imagination-inspiring and fun as our American Halloween holiday! This is the third book in a series in which I am trying to share today's Halloween with the reader. Neither the ancient mystical religious holiday of Halloween's past, nor the ancient holiday celebrated by Pagans and Wiccans worldwide is explored. The Halloween delved deeply into here is the fondly remembered enchanting evening, full of the innocence of childhood and the mystery of Love, graced with the fantasy that Mother Nature's special autumnal wand produces!

Just as we all love Santa Claus, regardless of religious preferences, Halloween is celebrated by most Americans as a harvest festival. It is a fun and scary time, a holiday that is uniquely American. I do not feel it is necessary to dwell upon ancient Celts and Druids. Today's neo-pagans that I have spoken with are quite happy that the whole country is enjoying their holiday with them, even though for different reasons. Therefore, I do not feel I am slighting anyone by taking a different road and seeing things in a less serious, more child-like way. I have often been to Stonehenge, Avebury and the wonderful "Druidic" sites; however, I do not feel going into the archeology of Salisbury Plain, as fascinating as it is, is the nucleus of our holiday. There are many wonderful books on paganism and on the early stone circles, monoliths, etc. Those who feel these sites sacred and blessed are quite happy to indulge us in our more child-like pursuits. Our modern day Halloween, like Saint Patrick's Day, has very little in common with its roots in ancient days.

The seeds may have come from across the sea in Celtic lands but Halloween, as we celebrate it, is a truly American holiday. I can not emphasize this enough. The Scottish bard Robbie Burns inspired us. Yet, it was not until those transplanted poems—carried from Scotland to the new world by immigrants—took root in American culture, that they slowly grew and matured into the field of fantasy we know today as Halloween. We cannot emphasize enough how important Robert Burns' two poems are for their influence on Halloween. Read these two poems to learn about the roots of today's Halloween.

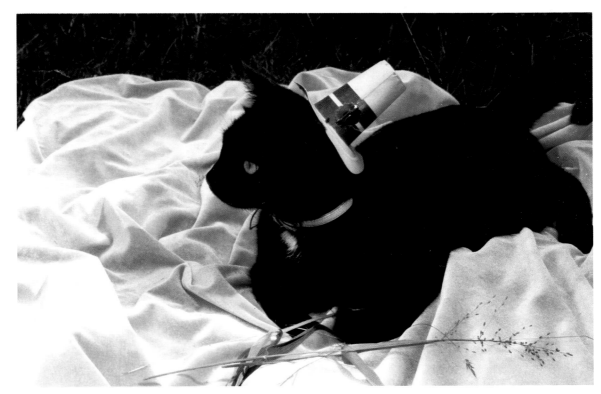

Bahron Muhrchoom, the Magnificent, sitting in the yard is the not so silent partner in Chris Russell and the Halloween Queen. It is his job to approve of all items and people who approach his kingdom. Starting life feral, he was found by Rescue and, after a few months of living in Trick or Treat Land and visiting the vets almost once a week, has become healthy and happy, terrorizing everyone with his friendliness and demands to be loved. He exercises this right even on the Veggie people!

Stonehenge cast dimensional figure. This is how it must have looked at one time with the moon light shining down on it and the ghosts of ancient Druids flittering amongst the ruins. If you have never seen Stonehenge, you are missing one of the great wonders of the world.
Gift from Jill and Derek Popplestone

Druids alter, Island Magee Larne Co., Antrim. This postcard show the ancient stones in front of a building. *Gift from Alf Harris*

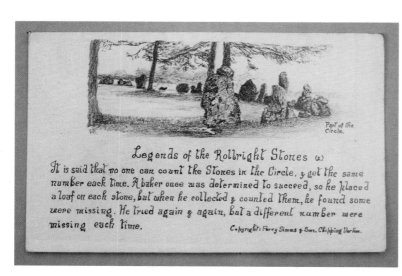

Two postcards of the legend of the Rollrights stones. Cards like these were hardly collected years ago; but, now archeologists, neo-druids, and local history buffs seek out cards of the different great stones. When I first started collecting these, long ago, I made the mistake of putting down on a postcard club roster that I collected the great stones, which they then put down as "Big Rocks!" Hardly the same thing, but it has given us many a laugh. Cards like these are worth approximately $4 ea. *Gift from Alf Harris and Richard Moulton.*

"The Temple at Avebury, a restoration after J. Briton" shows how the greatest of the stone circles looked. Rather awesome in its majesty.
Gift of Alf Harris and Richard Moulton

Postcard of the inner circle of Stonehenge. *Gift from Dr. Richard Moulton*

Of Halloween Today, This Book, and Collecting

This book is a companion to *Collectible Halloween* and *More Halloween Collectibles*. There are so many wonderful items that have been made during the twentieth century that we have tried not to duplicate here. The intention here is to show those items we have not been able to share with you before. The chapters, as in a novel, go on, leading us from one exciting aspect to another, sometimes backtracking, sometimes overlapping, but seldom repeating. The quantites of items made over more than one hundred years is vast. Even if I wrote twenty books, it would hardly touch on all the marvelous fantasy items created for our holiday.

Behind each autumn colored leaf is a pixie, behind every tree trunk is excitement, and on the whispers and howls of the wind are dreams. They are dreams of fantasy, dreams of being, for one night, someone or some*thing* else. Childhood is made of dreams and, if we are lucky, when we grow older we retain those dreams. Then Halloween becomes even more important to us as a means of maintaining those sparks of childish delight, a hint of immortality.

Halloween has for thirty years filled my life with joy. The joy at seeing children out trick or treating with their families. The joy of witnessing how much pleasure they shared with each other, and with us, whose homes were a Mecca to these costumed celebrants. The joy of sharing my collection with friends I have made, who collect and celebrate my favorite holiday. Joy at being privileged to being told memories and

stories by people who had almost forgotten them but remembered and so captured a bit of the innocence of their youth. Joy at knowing that, while once I as a collector was once considered a bit of a nut or an eccentric, I am now being touted as a visionary of sorts. A visionary with pumpkin people dancing in my head perhaps, but a visionary for falling in love with a fantasy that blocks out the harshness of the world the newspapers tout each day.

I am truly grateful for the joys of Halloween and, therefore, I feel I must share these joys with all of you. With over ten thousand items in my collection, I have been able to slowly start documenting some of the wonderful items that have sprung into being around Halloweens' past. In this book, I am also using one chapter to celebrate the talents of those who have kept the traditions alive. The talented individuals who make original Halloween items and add to the pleasure of today's collectors need to be recognized and thanked. Besides, the wares these folk artists produce are so affordable!

Collecting should be an inclusive thing. Not everyone has unlimited funds to indulge their every whim. Certainly I don't. I feel the beginning collector and those who cannot afford high dealer prices are as important as individuals whose collections are prestigious. The person who adds to a display every year, decorates with it, and then lovingly puts it away for another year is as much a part of the Halloween collecting community as those among us who keep collections up all year long and take every chance we can to play with them.

Salvador Dali said he was Surrealism. I say, you and I, collectors and trick or treaters, collectively are Halloween.

Prices

Prices are subjective. No two people look at an item and see it in the same light. It is written that the bat and the owl see the tree differently than the mouse and the fox. Well, perhaps I wrote that, but my pseudo Sufi sayings make a point. An items value depends on how you are looking at that item. Are you a collector, a dealer, a dealer collector, a celebrator, an investor, or a speculator? Do you really love the stuff and want to take it with you when you pass over? Are you building a collection while waiting for prices to go up, or until something else hits your fancy? Are you selling your duplicates like I do, or items you have found at a nice price, or are you out to squeeze ever single last bit of green out of the collector's pocket?

I have made my living as an antiques dealer for almost thirty years. The only reason I stay in business is that the same people come back to me week after week, year after year. I've always said, a fair price is the best price. Everyone loves a bargain or a steal. There is something very exciting about walking into a show or house sale and finding a piece priced so low it made your heart pound as you fumbled for your pennies to pay for it. Knowledge is a powerful thing and being in the right place at the right time sure helps.

So, what is the right price? It is different for everyone. If you can find an item readily for, let's say, $50, and the same piece is being sold by someone for $100, then obviously it is priced too high. On the other hand, if the same $50 item is priced at $20, pay the man or woman and bless them as you leave. One man's junk in another man's treasure.

The prices in this book are *my* prices. They are the prices I would sell the items for, if in stock, or what I would pay for them if I didn't already own them. They are the prices I see at the different shows, in the catalogues I receive, and from the auctions I attend. In other words, these prices are hybrids, conglomerations. This book is filled with a tossed salad of prices using common sense instead of lettuce.

Having done the Halloween sections for various price guides, I am amazed at the amount of mail I receive from people with items to sell that never take condition onto consideration. When I give a price, even for an example that is not perfect in the picture, I am pricing the item as if it were in excellent condition. Condition should be considered and price should be graded down relative to the wear and tear on the item. It is better always to own a less-than-perfect piece than not to own one at all. If everything had to be perfect, museums would be empty. Remember the Venus Di Milo is missing her arms! So, if an item has a bent corner, a scuffed surface, a missing bail, handle or face, you and only you have to grade that piece and determine if the price is fair to you. E-Bay has brought many items down in price, as have store finds. Common sense has to prevail, but you already know that.

Remember also that there are many reproductions and downright fakes out there and they are worth very little. I recently did an appraisal and was horrified to see that one dealer had consistently sold items that were brand new at prices that would have been high for old pieces. These were brand new items bought from a catalogue and the dealer knew it! There is quite a difference between brand new reproductions and vintage, old store stock. For the sake of your pocketbook, use your eyes and your mind. There are dealers who act like the worst of politicians of the ways and means committee variety. "If you have the means, we have the ways of taking it away from you!" is their creed.

So, after all is said and done, I have tried to give a fair price, fair to the seller and fair to the buyer. Sure, I'd love to give the prices I paid twenty to thirty years ago: jack-o'-lanterns, 25 cents to $1.50; candy containers, $2 to $5; Dennison Bogie books 50 cents; and Winch postcards that I bought for 25 cents and sold the duplicates for one dollar. How times have changed!

Use this book as a guide. It is after all, like any other guide, just a guide. It is someone's, in this case mine, opinion on a subject that they have spent considerable time ruminating over. In my case, these prices come from thirty years experience of pinching pennies and eating pasta in order to buy one more piece of orange and black that I scoured the country to find. Maybe thirty years from now I'll think today's prices cheap or maybe the world will have changed so much that nothing will have any value. Either way, the true value is in the question, "How much pleasure it gives me." Isn't your cat or dog worth more than the vet bill and the food you feed it? Mine is. So, get out your salt shaker when you look at price tags, any price tags, and then, after you've used your thinking caps, make your informed decision.

Halloween: A Discussion and a Look to the Future

Halloween, Exactly What Does It Encompass?

How do you decide what belongs in a Halloween collection and what doesn't? I'm often asked that question and I think, within reason, anything goes. Here is a case where I believe someone would be crossing the line between Halloween fantasy collecting and poor taste. I do not think it is proper for someone's skeleton to be pulled out of a medical school and propped up with a top hat for decoration. Most people would not want that done to them (Golden Rule), so in deference to those who have passed on and have not been consulted about their wishes, I do not feel they should be included in any Halloween doings. Halloween is for fantasy, not grim reality.

Haunted houses can get quite gory and scary and, though I know many people love them, I have never been into blood-soaked ghouls. They are too much like the evening news. That sort of horror has its place, I guess, and, though I do not include the gory and grotesque into my personal Halloween collection, it has its following. Mechanical maniacs murdering or mechanical electrocutions of monsters and men are a bit too gory for me.

Excuse my Disney mentality for a moment, but I have never thought the disgusting was scary. It is too much like being on a boat when people around you are suffering from mal de mere! Vincent Price and Alfred Hitchcock had it right, what is frightening comes from anticipation, your own mind, and your own fears. Don't open that door! Look out behind you (imagine the music from a scary movie playing here)! The foot steps are coming up the stairs and you have nowhere to hide, nowhere to run. Now that's scary!

While I adore ghost stories and tales of the macabre, I don't necessarily mix them all the time. It is for you to decide how much Gothic horror you want to incorporate into a collection. I adore Edward Gorey's work and I feel it fits in nicely, as I do *The Munsters, The Addams Family, Nightmare Before Christmas, Bewitched, Sabrina the Teenage Witch, Dark Shadows*, and similar genre.

Like most children, I found nothing scary about the Burton-Disney movie, *Nightmare Before Christmas*. It was romantic and sweet, and I even loved that bug eating, wormy villain, Oogie Boogie. A real T Rex in my back yard would be scary, an off worlder, maybe. So indulge yourself, add in each and every aspect of the holiday that you feel comfortable with. Your celebration will reflect you.

What This Book Encompasses

Most of the ten thousand items in our collection are not scary, but rather like a trip into an Arthur Rackham painting (of fairies, ghosties and wee spirits of the forest). You have seen some of that collection in the last two volumes and this one is more of the same ilk. In this book are table decorations, Ouija boards, and games—all the things you can use to decorate and/or entertain.

A word or two concerning the Ouija. I have heard horror stories of people who have had terrifying experiences with the Ouija. All I can say is that such folk have probably been watching too much late night television. If you do not like Ouijas, or they give you the creeps, don't own them and don't use them. I sort of feel that way about television. I don' t want one in the house ... suppose those little guys in there jump out with their guns, and knives, and evening news toupees! Jay walking is scary too, as is drinking and driving. I once heard of a friend of a friend's cousin's, cousin's, friend who was attacked by a gigantic spider that crept out of the screen, escaping from a nature film! Right!

As I said Halloween, should be fun, a multi-generational experience. So, who is the arch villain in your Halloween collection, Dracula or Darth Vader?

Enter into my world of Halloween, where the witches, fairies, and anthropomorphic vegetable and fruit people scamper about amidst the bright orange and green leaves. Shall I tell you a secret? Leprechauns and Santa's Elves are real. I know because they come trick or treating at my house!

Documentation and the Need For Research

Catalogues are excellent sources for the identification of items. So little information is available and so few companies have kept their records, assuming they are still in business, that it is very difficult to identify their products. The fire bombing of Dresden, Germany, during World War II, where many items were produced, wiped out most of the manufacturers' records. It is the rare item which has its original tag or packaging which will identify the maker or the artist. In rare cases, as in the cases of Biestle and Union Plastics, companies have had the foresight to keep their catalogues. So many companies were small, regional firms that often did not mark their items. Just because something looks like something, doesn't mean it is.

As a case in point, the Whitney pumpkin headed people look very much like the work of Rose O'Neil. There is no documentation or indication that she worked for Whitney or created these cards. So, who did? None of them are signed and all of Whitney's records went up in flames with the factory.

Tuck's records were destroyed when a bomb was dropped on the plant. Dennison, of Bogie Book fame, neglected to keep anything, a common habit among American companies. This lack of evidence makes it very difficult to attribute an item to a particular company or artist. Magazine ads are great for dating an item but this is still scanty information. Who made the products, who designed them, where were they made, and where were they sold, how much did they cost and who bought them? So many questions and so little information!

For the last year, we have been contacting people looking for sponsors to set up a full time museum. One of the most important parts of this undertaking will be documentation. Beside all the old catalogues and advertisements, we have tried to gather as many new catalogues as possible. With the new catalogues we are assured that, ten or twenty years from now, we will be able to document these "new" items.

Most people do not, assuming the item comes packaged, wish to keep that package. The packaging is identification and often has the retail price on it. Because Dennison's Bogie books were crafts books as well as catalogues for selling items,

they dated and identified their products. Napkins, stickers, seals, die cuts, crape paper, invitations, table clothes, and the like can be found between the pages of these priceless booklets. Catalogues, even if they have only one page of Halloween items, are important documentation. Much of our information is gathered from these booklets and pamphlets.

Photographs have been another valuable information source. Photos of Halloween parties, and people in costume, sometimes show decorations, lanterns and candy containers. A picture of your aunt Samantha at the age of seven in 1926 holding a particular lantern dates the item and also indicates it was sold in a particular area. Assuming that they do not go out of business, it would behoove companies to keep an archive for posterity or to deposit these items with a museum.

I, for one, am always delighted when I see an item in its original packaging with, say, a ten cent Woolworth's price tag on it. Sometimes, the excitement of finding the price tag overshadows finding the item.

Unlike their predecessors at the turn of the twentieth century, who rarely marked their wares, folk artists and crafts people are signing their work today. Professional photographers and artists are capitalizing on a popular Halloween theme and foreign countries are producing items, sometimes for themselves but mostly for the American market.

I personally, have an ethical problem with buying new items made in certain countries or imported by certain large corporations, because of their use of child labor and the payment of slave wages. I guess this is one of the reasons I am so excited about the revival of folk artists, those cottage industry entrepreneurs upon whose labors this country was founded.

The Southern potters have produced wonderful jugs with Devil faces. I guess they associate the devil and the drink, as these jugs were originally used for keeping whiskey. Still, these jugs are so perfect for Halloween that I could not resist them. Why would I?

The Japanese have adopted Halloween wholeheartedly and *Nightmare Before Christmas* became so big in Japan that all types of items have been newly licensed. These are items you will have to buy on the secondary market, from someone in Japan, or from a toy dealer who is importing them. There are some dynamite items among them which will be addressed in a future book.

Fortune Telling and Halloween

It is almost impossible to separate fortune telling from Halloween. Halloween is the night to have your fortune told, so you will know who your mate will be, or if you are doomed to spend another year loveless and forlorn! Gypsies and fortune tellers, real and make believe, have dominated the imagination about this holiday since its inception. Reread Robert Burn's poem "Halloween" (it may be found in *Collectible Halloween*) and you will see how important knowing "if he loves you and will be true or if she will be a good mate and make you happy" was to those lovers generations ago. Times have not changed; Love still makes the world go round! Among the games of love and chance, one of the greatest larks, still, is having your fortune told. Read the poems on the postcards and you will see the fortune theme runs throughout.

Halloween is a night to predict the future to see into the days after tomorrow. I'll predict something for you right now. As long as you keep the essential innocence of Halloween in your heart, you will be a happier and healthier person. However, don't put this book down on your taxes as a medical expense or you'll get in big trouble!

The Future Of Halloween

I truly feel that (despite the vocal minority sentiment against Halloween and its revelers) the holiday is in safe hands, yours and mine, and will therefore prosper. We are at present looking for sponsors and investors for a full time museum in the Salem, Massachusetts, area. I feel this will be healthy for all of us.

No one is too old to celebrate Halloween. More stores are carrying Halloween items, more magazines are covering the holiday positively—as it should be covered—and more people are becoming aware of what a wonderful family oriented entertainment it is. Celebrating Halloween is something like finding yourself on a stage or movie set. It is up to you if you want to be part of the crowd scene, be a star, or direct the production!

I feel very sad when people tell me that, in their school or neighborhood, Halloween parades are banned or that Trick or Treating is not allowed. These children are being denied one of the great delights of childhood. Those who don't want to participate shouldn't but I, for one, do not intend to be denied the joys of the night or of giving out treats to the neighbor's children. I know there are tens of thousands of others who feel the same way and that is why so much candy and so many decorations are bought every year.

Every year, more people in other countries discover Halloween. Whenever large department and toy stores, whatever the nationality, find they can make money supplying people with holiday accouterments, additional consumers discover Halloween. I was so excited the year I found a whole section of decorations in Harrod's of London!

The Scandinavians are pulling out their Christmas and Easter witches and decorating while the Russians are dusting off old Baba Yar. From Mexico, the Day of the Dead is spreading to the states and wafting back upon them like a wave, returning with it our celebratory traditions. Today, and for the foreseeable future, Halloween is alive (a strange word to use in this context) and well. Like a giant Tsunami, it is rising and swelling, spreading cheer everywhere. Happy Halloween!

Noise Makers and Audio Effects

The howling of the wind, the moaning of ghosts, the laughter of children, the squeals of delight, the screams of the startled and the noise of ratchets and ear deafening noise makers are all among the sounds of Halloween. Make much noise and you will scare the goulies and ghosties and long legged beasties away!

Tin handle and frame with paper center and metal and wood clapper combination, which tended, unless owned by a gentle child, to be destroyed rather promptly. $45.

Below:
Cat with composition head and wood body. Ratchet noise maker. $75.

Paper face, wooden rim and stick. Bells on string made the noise but also tore the paper faces. Germany. $75.

Two paper and cardboard horns with wooden mouth bits and rims. German. $75 ea.

Unless the original owner of this banjo knew how to play it, it would give new meaning to the word noise maker. Complete with its own pick. $150.

Three wooden horns. $25 ea.

Wooden ratchet. $45.

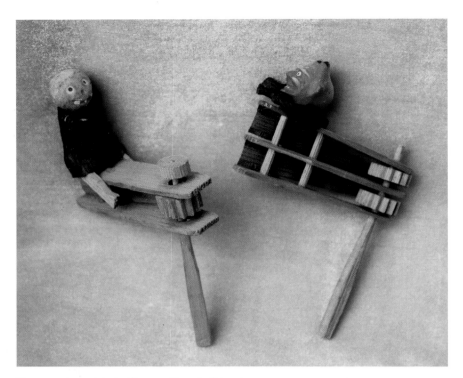

Two wooden ratchets. Composition devil head, double ratchet and composition jack-o'-lantern man with cloth covered wooden body. $125 ea.

Triple ratchet of wood with composition cat and jack-o'-lantern man rider, who has a crepe covered wooden body. $175.

Two German rattles of wood with paper faces. Small pebbles inside would make noise, and eventually destroy the item. $75 ea.

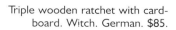

Triple wooden ratchet with cardboard. Witch. German. $85.

Wooden ratchet with composition head. Jaw of skeleton is hinged so that, as ratchet motion is in effect, the jaw would also move and would make a slight noise. $75.

These German cardboard noise makers, with paper inserts, have metal strikers. $12 ea.

Two early wooden ratchets with composition heads. The single ratchet (left) has a wooden body. $125. Double ratchet, $65.

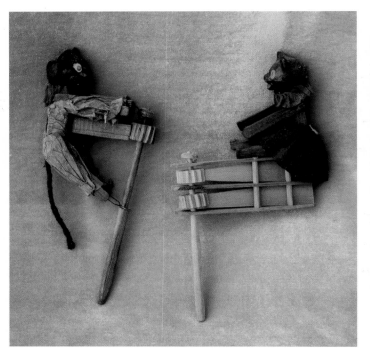

Two wooden ratchets with cats. Composition heads, wooden bodies, crepe covered. $145 ea.

Two cardboard horns with wooden mouthpieces. One has a wooden handle that is attached to a ratchet mechanism on the inside. 1931 Marks Bros. of Boston. Horn only, $20. Horn-ratchet, $25.

Four cardboard horns. $20 ea.

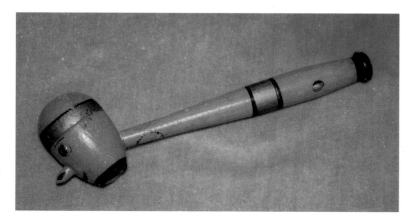

Wooden pipe noise maker. $65.

Three paper and cardboard candy containers on sticks. The candy, when shaken, would make the noise. $20 ea.

Wooden ratchet with composition, mushroom capped jack-o'-lantern man with wooden body and crepe clothing. $150.

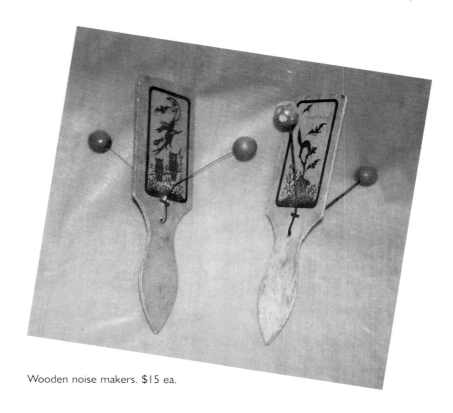

Wooden noise makers. $15 ea.

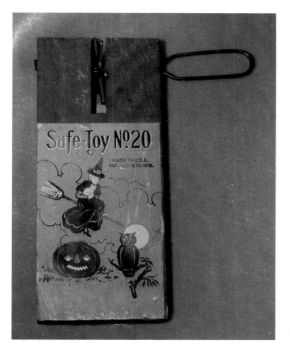

Safe Toy No 20. Made in USA 1918. Paper label over wood with metal ratchet workings. $35.

Wooden quadruple ratchet with German jack-o'-lantern cardboard face. $85.

Cardboard horn with a wooden tip, inserted through a wooden rimmed, paper faced drum. German made. $75 ea.

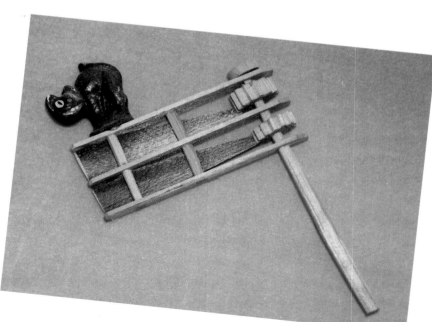

Composition cat on double wooden ratchet. $65.

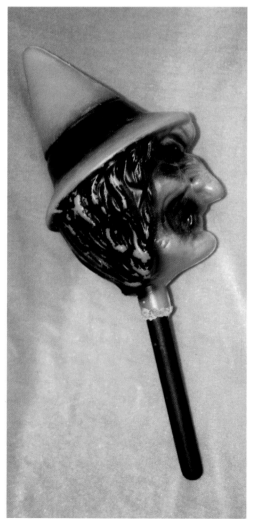

Plastic witch rattle on wooden stick with pebbles inside. $95.

Two wooden ratchets with pressed cardboard, German, jack-o'-lantern faces. $95 ea.

Cardboard horn with wooden head. $55.

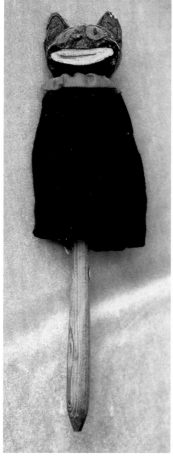

Composition cat head with cloth dress over wooden stick which, when shaken, doesn't make much noise but just moves about a bit. $85.

Two wood rattles with paper faces. The cat has a crepe ruffle top to simulate a fan effect. $95 ea.

Pressed board head and stem with a wooden bit and paper hair. This horn is unusual in shape. $125.

Two shakers: jack-o'-lantern with crepe skirt, witch with a candy box content noisemaker. $20 ea.

Paper horn from 1921. $35.

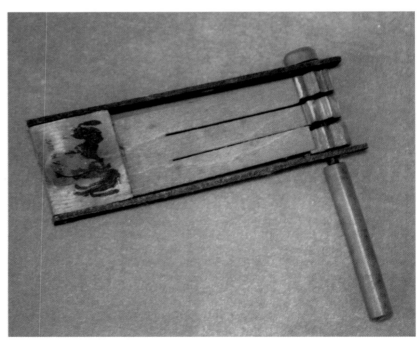

Wooden ratchet. $15.

Paper blower horns: the small one has a wooden mouth piece while the large one has a paper cat face. Small blower, $4. Cat blower, $12.

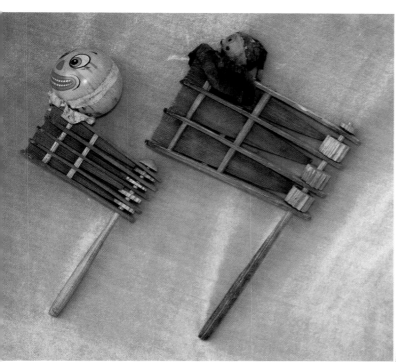

Two wooden ratchets: (left:[the jack-o'-lantern]) one with a composition head, $95; and (right:[jack-o'lantern with hat and dress]) one with a pressed paper German head, $125.

Paper face, wooden mouth piece and tissue dress, noise maker. $15.

Long paper horn and shorter horn with a wooden mouth piece. $25 ea.

Crepe and paper noise maker, reverse shows wooden clapper underneath. $20.

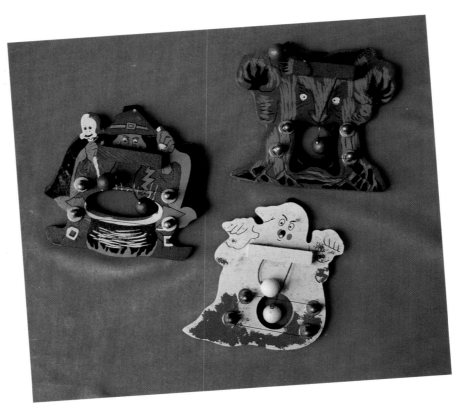

Three wooden noise makers, modern. $3 ea.

Flossie Fisher's Funnies

"Flossie Fisher's Funnies" was a children's page by illustrator Helene Nyce, who drew silhouette figures. Her "Funnies" appeared in *Ladies Home Journal* magazine and had a monthly contest to give the children a chance to win a one dollar prize!

The page was popular enough that china novelties and tin candy containers were made using Nyce's designs. The bright yellow background with black silhouettes of children are very appealing, but one wonders "why not an orange background." The jack-o'-lantern and children bobbing for apples shows the fun activities of autumn and Halloween.

The tin candy containers are shaped like doll house furniture. We have not included them in this chapter as all the examples we have been offered have been repainted or overpriced. We have, therefore, not been able to incorporate them into our collection.

Fisher's appeal is classic. Though the pieces are scarce, their charm has been overlooked for much too long. The magazine sheet is, of course, in black and white.

The funnies themselves, a magazine page. $12.

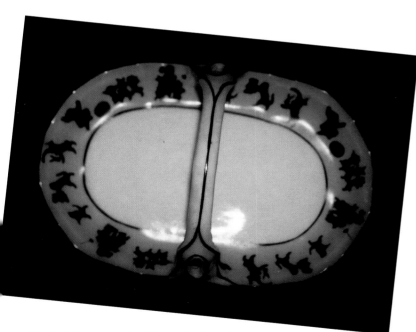

A basket shaped candy dish, made of good quality Victoria China, from Austria. $65.

Sugar bowl of fine china made in Austria by Victoria. $35.

Cup and saucer, Victoria
China, Austria. $85.

Right and below:
Pastry-sized plate, and a larger plate. Made in
Austria by Victoria China. Pastry plate, $35; and
larger plate, $55.

Winsch Halloween Postcards

To many postcard collectors, the John Winsch Halloweens are the creme-de-la-creme of all Halloween postcards. Certainly, the artwork of artist Samuel Schmucker is a fresh and exciting revitalization and Americanization of the Art Nouveau movement. The colors are vibrant, the women are bewitching, and the printing is excellent. Schmucker is not the only artist that Winsch published, but he is the most important.

Jason Freixas's, another wonderful Winsch artist, children are stylized and wide-eyed, which make them very easy to recognize. These artfully rendered children are another reason the Winsch name means so much.

Prices on these cards will range from $35 to $350, depending on rarity, whether they are copyright by Winsch, and where they were printed. Winsch Publishing was located in New York but did their printing in Germany because it was less expensive and of superior quality. Copyright Winsch cards predate America's entry to W.W.I, whereas cards without copyright appear to postdate the war and may have been produced as late as the 1920s.

The artwork was later rearranged, mocked up, and printed again by an unknown Bavarian printer. This anonymous printer used a pseudo-Winsch back on the cards.

The Schmucker women are the most desirable. Often, the most common cards have the largest and most stunning images! Remember, condition is important. When buying, grade the card for condition.

4 invitations with original envelopes. $145 ea. (Prices on E-Bay may be as much as three times higher.)

Schmucker. Girl in pine tree with owls.
$150, $125, $150, $150.

Because this is not a book on postcards, we are not showing all of the sets complete. However, there are enough postcards here so you can see the variations and changes and some of the stunning artwork. When newly off the press, these cards were the best examples of high art being made affordable and available to the general public, and they remain so. Collectors, during the golden age of postcards, treasured these cards, (hence so many have survived in excellent condition), as we do today. They were fortunate enough, however, to buy them mint off the racks while we must search, competing with collectors world-wide who acknowledge the artistic merit of publisher Winsch. Schmucker also created one Halloween set for Tuck Publishing and another for Whitney Publishing. Schmucker's art is the penultimate in fantasy.

For those desiring a complete listing of Winch Halloween cards, there is a check list by "Witch Hazel" Leler. This list may be obtained from the Gotham Book Mart in New York City.

Because variations can be rare, and because they are so interesting grouped together, I have grouped variations by images, taking the central figure as the nucleus. Notice how the central figure is reused over and over, even mixing artists' works together. One wonders if the central figures were not done and then the backgrounds composed by a lesser artist well versed in paste up.

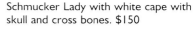

Schmucker Lady with white cape with skull and cross bones. $150

Left and far left:
More of the Schmucker Lady with white cape with skull and cross bones.
$125, $150.

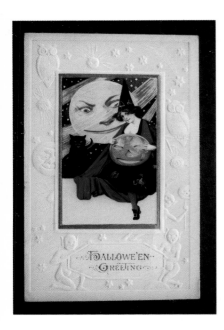

Beautiful witch with red cape holding jack-o'-lantern. $150, $110, $110.

Witch in elfish costume with wand releasing imps. Schmucker. $125, $150, $145, $125.

Lady in black starred dress with jack-o'-lantern man sweetheart. Schmucker. $175, $125.

This has got to be the most romantic of all the Schmucker cards. A beautiful woman sleeps, dreaming of her love while fairies protect her. $125 ea.

Little girl in white frock with masks. Schmucker. $125, $145.

Witch flying on broom with moon behind
her. Schmucker. $125, $95, $95, $95.

Woman in red dress with owl hat, sitting
on jack-o'-lantern. $150, $100.

Woman in white hooded outfit with red jack-o'-lanterns. Schmucker mask and jack-o'-lantern background. $145 ea.

Beautiful Schmucker witch with cauldron and scary faces in the background. $125, $135. (see right and below).

Woman sitting on pumpkin in the sky, being paid homage to by celestial jack-o'-lantern men. $110.

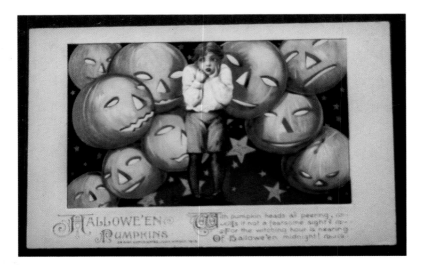

Perplexed Schmucker boy
with jack-o'-lanterns in sky.
The variation is a gelatin finish.
$75 ea.

Woman and man trying to play a game by
biting into a hanging heart. Schmucker.
$75.

Beautiful witch holding candle
with imps in background.
Schmucker. $125.

Woman in jack-o'-lantern with broom. Schmucker. $125.

Girl and boy carrying jack-o'-lanterns in their hands. $150, $300, $150.

Girl and boy, usually together, carrying brooms with jack-o'-lanterns hanging from them. $125, $150, $150, $150, $150, $300, $150.

Hallowe'en Pumpkins.

Hallowe'en Pumpkins

A Jolly Hallowe'en

The Hallowe'en Lantern

DESIGN COPYRIGHTED, JOHN WINSCH.

Girl and boy play with
jack-o'-lantern. $125,
$150, $150.

Girl and boy huddled together looking into sky.
Schmucker. $125, $125, $125, $125, $300, $125.

Witch flying on owl while her friends fly on bats. Five
variations. $100, $95, $150, $95, $125.

Six variations of a witch driving a corn mobile through the sky. $125, $95, rest $125 ea.

Witch and her veggie friends drive in anthrapomorphized
motor vehicle. Five variations. $125 ea.

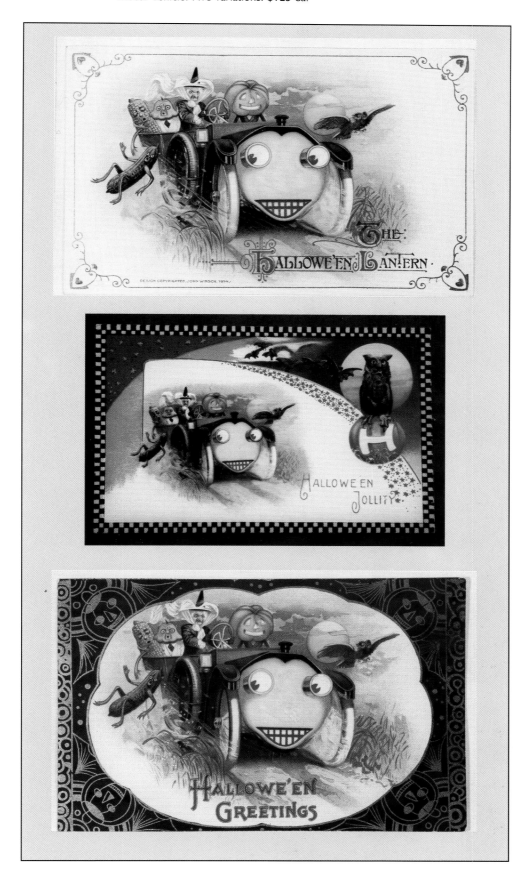

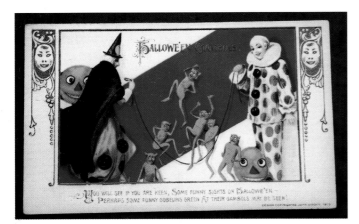

Witch and clown playing jump rope
with green beings. $135.

Two clowns with jack-o'-lantern jack
in the box. $110.

Four variations of witch in basket with ghost, and dangling veggie beings. $135 ea.

Startled little Freixas girl with jack-o'-lantern men in the sky. $85.

Schmucker girl in sky with red, bat riding beings. $85.

Little girl on bat in the sky with her dog and red beings. Freixas. $110.

Little girl running from jack-o'-lantern headed boy. $110.-

Little boy bringing jack-o'-lantern in a wheel barrow to little girl with dog. Note the Schmucker fairies in the window. $110.

Boy with mask scaring Freixas girl. Notice Schmucker red imp-being in corner. $110.

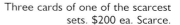

Three cards of one of the scarcest sets. $200 ea. Scarce.

Schmucker fairies and cat with jack-o'-lantern. $110.

Little Freixas girl with jack-o'-lantern and puppet. Witch in moon. $110.

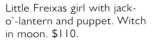

Perplexed girl with cigar smoking jack-o'-lantern man. Perplexed boy with owl and dog. (Some children just don't know what to make of all the strange goings on.) $150 ea.

Freixas boy with jack-o'-lantern, above him is a cat in a haystack and a flying moon. $110.

Cat in haystack with flying owl and witch in moon. This is definitely a composite of two other cards. $75.

Freixas girl in her pajamas with jack-o'-lantern. $110.

Freixas boy with jack-o'-lantern on stick. $110.

Jack-o'-lantern man
dances with Freixas
boy. $110.

Freixas girl looks at owl, moon,
and jack-o'-lantern. $110.

Left and above:
Woman in white carries jack-o'-
lantern past two owls in a tree. $95,
$110.

Freixas child removing lid from jack-o'-lantern. $100, $100, $125.

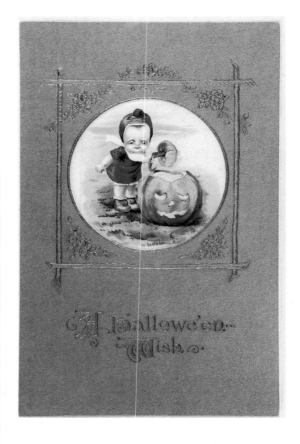

Freixas girl kicking and rolling an unhappy jack-o'-lantern. $100, $100, $100, $125.

Freixas girl on jack-o'-lantern. This kitten really gets around. $100 ea.

Beautiful woman sits in jack-o'-lantern sedan, carried by two green beings. $95.

Schmucker woman carries a candle, while looking behind her at the clock. $95.

Lovely woman dances a light fantastic with jack-o'-lantern headed broom. $95.

Freixas girl looks at witch flying out of steaming jack-o'-lantern. $100, $100, $125.

Schmucker lady with two jack-o'-lantern smokers. These two guys really get around! $75.

Schmucker woman sits holding jack-o'-lantern on stick. $75.

Schmucker lady sits at corn stocks with clown behind her. Owl, frog, cats, witches—seems like everyone wants to find out what she is dreaming of! $110.

Owl with dancing pumpkin headed haystacks. This kitten sure looks familiar. $45.

Puritan-looking Schmucker lady in corn field with pumpkins. $65 ea.

Schmucker girl dances with owl and jack-o'-lantern man. $125.

Schmucker woman in black celestial gown. Jack-o'-lantern moon behind her. $110.

Arcade Machines and Mechanical Figures

It is so easy to become fascinated by moving, mechanical items. In the early days, the larger items were seen in amusement parks and arcades. Such objects have now disappeared into private collections. Large arcade machines are wonderful to own but difficult to repair or service. When you find a good one, you have a gem indeed but beware of replaced parts, repaints, and fakes.

In the movie *Big*, the Zoltan fortune telling machine was made of wood and was older than the fiberglass version we show; but, it is interesting to see the later version. Arcade machines hold a fascination for nostalgia seekers who remember them from the theme parks of their youth. They tend to be expensive, however, which helps explain the increasing popularity of smaller, battery operated items we will explore next. Of course, you can get into the super-scarce automaton and designer specials like those made as movie props, but then you are literally buying art, art of a macabre sort.

The battery operated items have made a real revival of late, with companies like Motion-ette producing some wonderful items; objects everyone can incorporate quite easily into a collection without too much effort or expense. Many new Halloween items that move, speak, laugh, cackle, crow, light up or flap their wings show up in stores every year during the fall months. Collecting these one could spend a fortune on batteries, but they are such fun.

The Wizard Fortune Teller. For one cent you could have your fortune told. This is a prime example of a fortune machine. The cast aluminum front has all its original paint. The case is wood and the inside wheel is paper. Be very careful, as these are often repainted or, worse still, the cast face is not original. $3500.

Zoltan arcade machine, fiberglass case. Remember the movie *Big*? $2000.

A swanky diner probably used this chrome Swami fortune and napkin dispenser. $125.

Postcard advertising the Swami napkin and fortune dispenser. $20.

Old time chrome diners would have sported this type of napkin/fortune dispenser with bright chrome. Painted aluminum plaque. $160.

Modern Snoopy mechanical toy that dances to the music and lights up his crystal ball. Schultz's character is so lovable. Snoopy makes a rocking good wizard! Lucy is a witch, and Charlie Brown a Vampire, and boy can they rock! It's amazing what a squeeze of a hand can do. $25 ea.

This came from the arcade at Circus World in Florida. The Palm Reader cardboard sign only dates from the forties, but the oak machine is older. Top only is shown here and the base is of matching oak. It was full of Exhibit Supply Co.'s cards, which you could purchase for five cents. Not a bad price to find out who you would marry and if that marriage would be successful! $400.

Battery operated Dracula in coffin with original box. $25.

Sound activated vampire with original box. $35.

Battery operated vampire, 10", more silly than scary. $20.

Rocking Witch with box by Gemmy Industries. $30.

Mystery Door Knocker in original package. $15.

Vincent the Living Skull, battery operated. $25.

Motion-ettes, witch with original box. $20.

Houston Gumball Machine with original box. $14.

She has that horrible cackle that children seem to love. $20.

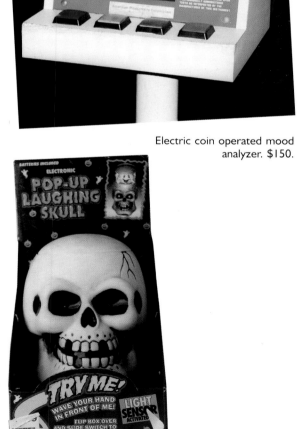

Electric coin operated mood analyzer. $150.

Left and far left: Pop-Up Laughing Skull in original box. Light sensitive. $15.

Electric, coin operated astrology fortune dispenser by Mutuscope. $400.

This Early "Raise the Devil Out of Hell" machine came from the now defunct, Circus World. It is a strength machine. Two grown men tried, and the best they could do was raise him high enough for you to see his head at the very bottom! Wood, glass and metal. $400.

Motion-ette ghost with box. $75.

Motion-ette vampire with box. This guy needs a good dentist and a good barber! $75.

Motion-ette witch with box. $75.

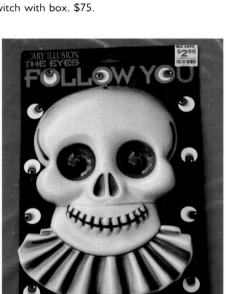

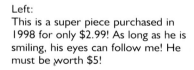

An alien fortune teller. The alien figure is easing his way into the Halloween world. Cute but not mystical, sci-fi, a "could almost be." $20.

Left:
This is a super piece purchased in 1998 for only $2.99! As long as he is smiling, his eyes can follow me! He must be worth $5!

Coffin Bank with box ...Oops, there goes another penny. $20.

Motion-ette box not shown. Mary Shelley would be surprised how her monster has dumbed down over the years. $75.

Table Decorations: Plates, Napkins, Table Covers, Party Favors, Candles, Place Cards, Teapots and Other Items Used on a Halloween Table

Teapots and Cups

Halloween is a party and parties mean food, glorious food. What better way to present that food in a festive manner than to turn the harvest table into a decorative delight of autumnal colors and anthropomorphic vegetables, fruits, and animal figures. It is unfortunate that today we do not take as much care and delight in producing a table that looks like it came out of a posh gourmet magazine. Years ago, one of the important aspects of Halloween involved a suitor coming to a girl's house and discovering what a great homemaker he was wooing. Today, both men and women cook and keep house. The inventive ones love Halloween. It gives them such a wonderful chance to be creative, showing off both their culinary and decorative skills.

Remember, Halloween and the full moon are made for candlelight suppers! It's a great time for proposals and is increasingly popular for weddings. Saint Matrimony would be so pleased!

Polite society, from the Victorian age to today, adores inviting in a Gypsy, Russian, or someone with an exotic accent to read their fortunes, at fancy teas served by French maids in Victorian mansions. It was very chic. It was very sophisticated. In the Middle East, it is still a very popular pastime, and some of those fortune tellers are very accurate!

Fortune telling is a very old profession. Every country that had tea or coffee would incorporate the reading of the leaves or grinds. To this day, when we make the thick sweet Armenian powdered coffee at home, my Dad will ask my mother or I to read the grinds. This kind of reading is part of many cultures and the more you do it, the better you get. It is fun and it is interesting and so are the collectibles depicting it. Teapots and cups can be very decorative and fit in beautifully with every decor. They are part of Halloween entertaining and belong on the Halloween table.

When the leaves clung to the porcelain, their positions would determine the reading. "The Cup of Knowledge." $45.

A Gypsy fortune telling cat spreading out the cards. The cat is reminiscent of Violet Roberts's cats. The teapot is English and most certainly would be used to serve tea that would leave a few leaves in the cup to be read. $200.

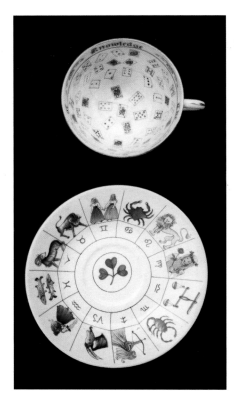

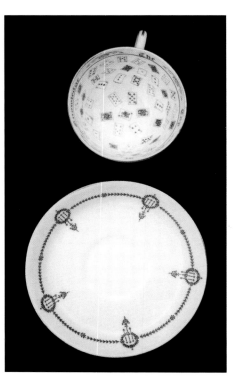

A Zodiac cup and saucer. $40.

This porcelain "Cup of Knowledge" is interesting because it has a Zodiac saucer. $40.

A rather plain saucer for "A Cup of Knowledge." $35.

These two women, in Welsh national costume, were probably witches because they were good looking and read their tea leaves (tongue in cheek). The poor witch had so many persona and, because of her hat, many people couldn't tell the difference between the Welsh and the witch. This is very upsetting to both the Welsh and the witches, but doesn't seem to bother Welsh Witches. $12.

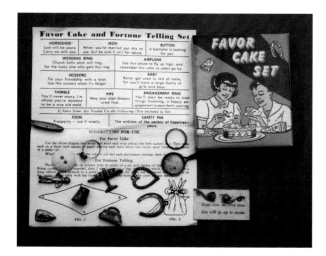

Tea could be a rather formal affair and small sweet cakes were always served. These small trinkets would be put into each petite sweet. This set was given by Breyers Ice Cream. Each trinket meant something. If you found a ring, that meant marriage on the near horizon, a button meant a bachelor, a shoe good luck, etc. $45.

Favor cake sets were as much fun for children as they were for adults. It was a case of "taster beware," however, as you could end up swallowing your favor by accident, or worse still, breaking a tooth with it. $45.

Fortune telling cake sets like these were not just used for Halloween, but for many occasions. These items certainly wouldn't be used today, especially the ones with paint on them. $45.

Sheet music, *In A Little Gypsy Tea Room*, Joe Burke with lyrics by Edgar Leslie. $20.

Booklet, *Your Future In The Tea Cup*, 1935, 24 pages, advertising Lipton's Tea. $15.

Good fortune as told by tea or coffee grounds. "Ring—A Happy Marriage." $10.

Holmes and Edwards advertising card. $8.

An old photograph, not faded as this is how it was taken, with sunlight flooding into the room. Notice to the right there is almost a spectral figure behind one of the women! $45.

The shapes a reader sees affect the reading. $7.

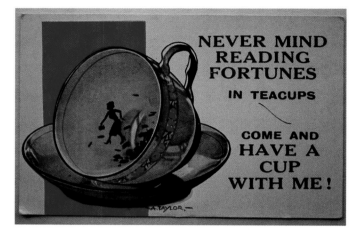

Taylor's sentiment told it all, friendship and camaraderie are what really counts. $8.

This postcard is by artist Fred Lounsbury. $8.

Royal Doulton creamer showing a witch working at her cauldron. $65.

Exhibit Supply Co., 1934 fortune card. $8.

Plastic plate made for McDonalds. $8.

This is a wonderful Royal Doulton coffee pot showing a scene from Robert Burns's poem "Halloween." The girls and boys are sitting about, roasting nuts. Depending on how the nut popped or burnt foretold whether you would marry that year or if your love would be true. $400.

Four paper cups that match up with plates, napkins, or table covers. $6 ea.

This Goss trivet is perfect for the Halloween table as it has a wonderful grace by Robert Burns. "Some have meat and can not eat, and some would eat that want it. But we have meat and we can eat and so the Lord be thanked." Perfect for a harvest festival. $50.

Halloween Dixie cup. $3.

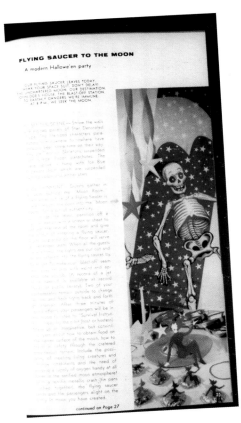

"Flying Saucers to the Moon a modern Halloween party." A page from a Dennison mixed events party book showing a nice table setting. $25.

Trick or Treat candy bag for individual treaters. $3.

Drake's Ring Dings with advertising for "Madison Scare Garden" and instructions how to get your Hallow Meanies toy. *Gift from Eddy and Lynton of Madison Scare Garden.* $1box; $12 toy.

Recipe of the Month Magazine, October 1935, showing a nicely decorated Halloween table. $25.

Halloween Decorations (with the original card). These decorations can make even the most boring sandwich or cupcake look festive. $45.

Sealtest suggested this table decor to magazine readers. $25.

"Pumpkin Party" page in a cookbook displays a festive Halloween table. $20.

Paper Plates

The lovely thing about these plates is that they make wonderful wall decorations. As pretty as a picture or a china plate.

Two cardboard dinner plates. $12 ea.

Square-shaped plates were in vogue in the '40s. $6 ea.

Package of six 8" Reed's Party Plates. $40.

Two paper plates. $10 ea.

Two dinner-sized plates. Fancy paper plates were, and are, often used by collectors as wall decorations. $12 ea.

Front and back of two different sized plates in the original packages, by Beach. $40 for 8". $30 for small size.

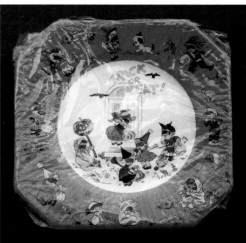

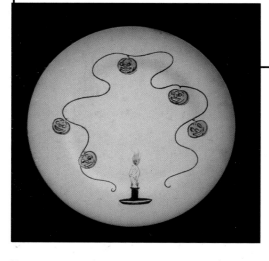

Round early (teens) paper plate. $15.

Two interesting dinner-sized paper plates. $12 ea.

Goosebumps plates, both sizes by Hallmark. These are very popular with today's young celebrators. $5 for the pair.

Two small-size, 6" paper plates representing the 1940s and the teens. Witch border, $6. Candle with jack-o'-lanterns, $10.

Modern day graphics are great fun and are being incorporated into many a collection. Party Creations. $3.

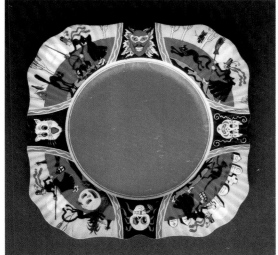

Front and Back of package of ten, 8 inch Smart-Set plates by Beach and Arthur, Inc. This is one of my favorites because the graphics are very deco in feel and the label is so large and informative. Matching napkins and tablecloths were made. And, they were non absorbent and color fast! $55. Single small size, $8.

8" plate. Do cats really sing on Halloween? $12.

8" plate. This cat either has been to the dentist or should have gone to one! $12.

Small plate. This may be Peter Pumpkin Eater's wife's house. $6.

8" plate. They used to put bricks of ice cream on plates like this and then throw them away. Ephemera! I'm glad they saved this one. $12.

6" plate. $6.

6" plate. $6.

6" plate. $6.

Round 6" plate. $6.

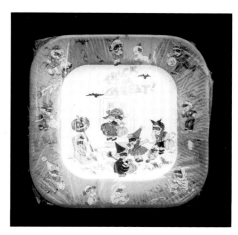

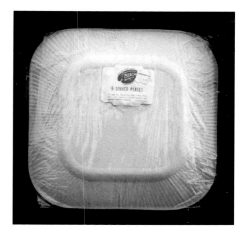

Front and back of 8" plates by Beach Original. The Woolworth's price tag is 15 cents! $60.

Front and back of 8" package of six plates by Reed's. $60.

McDonalds plastic plate. $20.

M.A. Hadley small butter pat size plate. $12.

Napkins

Now, wipe your mouth and fingers and don't get the cake on your costume...and there goes another piece of ephemera! It is amazing that so many of these napkins have survived. It must have been the graphics, or the fairies disguised them! Or the survival rate among napkins shows the universal reluctance of children to wipe either their faces or hands clean on anything other than sleeves or pants legs.

Paper tablecloths, plates and napkins are so ephemeral. They were made to be used once and then thrown away. Crape paper and tissue are fragile and it is amazing that so many people carefully stored away these items as if they were treasured heirlooms. As a collector, I can tell you that finding these items in their original packaging, with a price tag and the store name on them, is a great treat. However, don't pass up the single napkin or unpackaged item, because you might not find them in unused, packaged condition. Sometimes these items were kept to be cut up and used for decorations the next year; therefore, it was not important that there was a tear here and a stain there. After all, you would only cut out the figures or use the portions that would enhance your decorations anyway. Walls, costumes, or boxes could be turned into ambiance with little effort or expense.

Napkin with traditional Halloween motifs. $2.

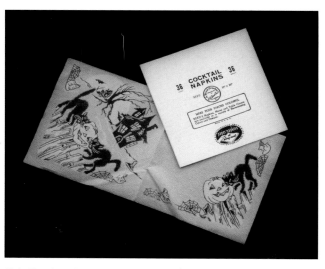

E.A. Reed cocktail napkin package. $20.

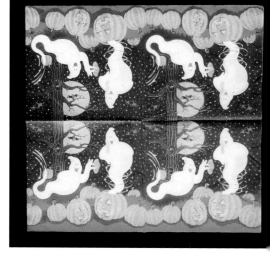

Modern napkin with a busy design. $1.

Two cocktail napkins. The one with the scarecrow is marked "Made in USA". Oh, for the good old days when some things were still made in America! $2 ea.

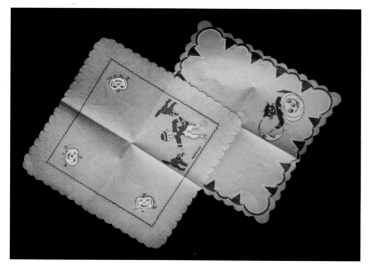

Early crepe type paper napkin. $10.

"Dennison's Crepe Paper Napkins" in original packaging. Dennison is the most important name in party decoration. They produced both quality items and the "Bogie books" that taught the reader how to decorate with their products. $20.

Napkin. $2.

Dennison's crepe paper napkins, with original packaging. Dennison's designs are rather distinctive. $20.

Two napkins, as different in style and design as one jack-o'-lantern is from another. $2 ea.

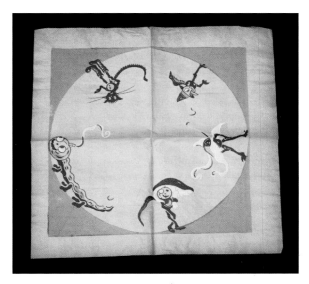

Napkin with fun fantasy figures. $2.

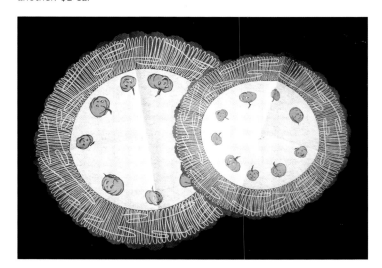

Napkin or plate cover. The graphics are both fun and different. $3 ea.

Two great napkins. $2 ea.

Napkin with cobweb center. $2.

Instead of an over all design, the artwork is all concentrated on the top of the folded section. A few bats, however, escaped. $2.

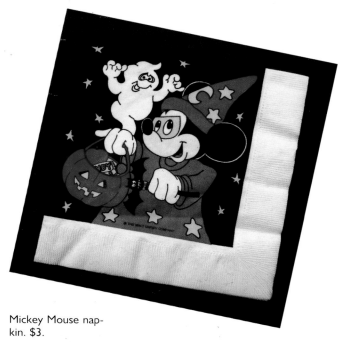

Mickey Mouse napkin. $3.

Two early crepe napkins. $10 ea.

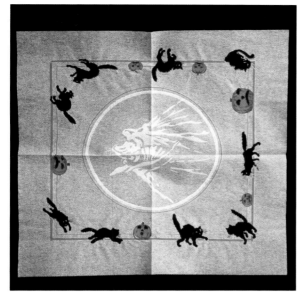

Table Cloths

Paper tablecloths seldom made it from one use to another. Soda and coffee was spilt on it, sticky fingers dropped sticky and sweet treats on it. Use it once and throw it away! Thanks heavens everyone didn't do that.

Two paper table covers in their original packaging. One by Hallmark and one by House of Paper. $15 ea.

A 54" x 96" table cover in its original packaging by Tuttle Paper Goods. The original 43 cent price tag is a hoot! When was the last time you saw an item priced at 43 cents? $35.

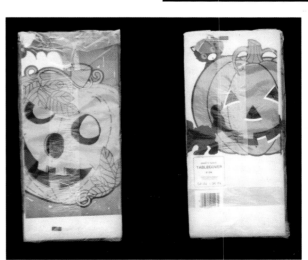

Two table clothes in original packaging, one with bar code. $15 ea.

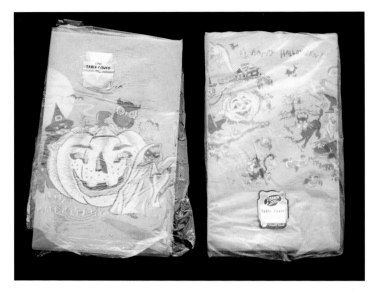

Two table covers in their original packaging. It is difficult to see the true colors of the cloths or the clarity of design under the original packaging, but most collectors prize such ephemeral items in their original state. $30 ea.

This table cloth is only bridge table size, but has a great fantasy design. $15.

Printed black design on orange may seem a bit busy, but it is stunning on a table. $25.

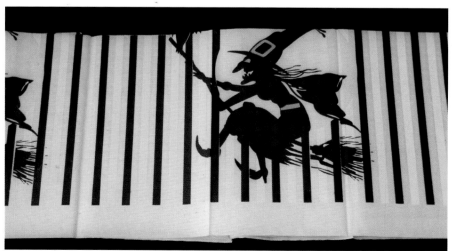

This rather mean looking witch makes an interesting tablecloth, especially with the green highlights. $25.

A wonderful frolic—rather busy and colorful. I don't think my cat would consider pulling a pumpkin cart! $25.

A charming table cover showing the love interest of two jack-o'-lantern beings. $25.

Paper table cloths usually had matching napkins. The napkin for this one is in the napkin section. $25.

Perkins table cover in original package. $30.

Candles

Where would the romance and the eerie flickers of shadow and light be if there were not candles on the table? Shaped candles by Gurley are the most desired but other companies made, and make, candles. They blend so well into a collection that one can not omit them. Again, on the whole, candles are still very affordable for the collector on a limited budget. Remember to keep these out of the sunlight and heat. Wax melts and, if softened, will distort its shape.

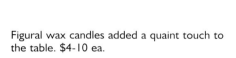

Figural wax candles added a quaint touch to the table. $4-10 ea.

Owl wax holder with inserted candle, meant to be burnt. A candle within a candle! $20.

Halloween Novelty Candles, Gurley store box. Suggested that they would make "swell party favors" and that they should be displayed in the candy section! $35.

Large candles, like this Gurley witch, were often used as centerpieces. Originally sold for 79 cents. $75.

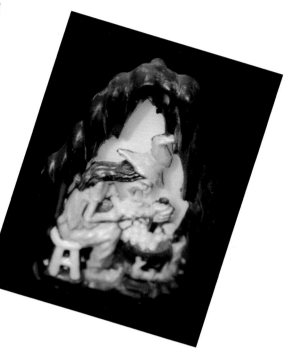

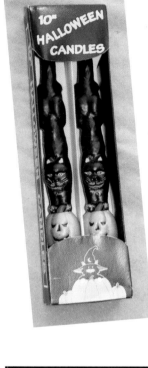

10" figural candles, in the original box. $12.

Witch's Brew Gurley Halloween Glow Candle, in original box. The candle is in the back and, when lit, it would flicker and make the witches cave seem like the fire was truly lit. $45.

Six candles, most of which are made by Gurley. $4-12.

Skull candle with spider on his head. $5.

Gurley witch and a later bear candle. Witch, $8; bear, $2.

Two pairs of 10" figural tapers. $12 ea. pr.

Two pairs of figural tapers. $12 ea. pr.

Six packages of Capri Candles from 1965 in their original boxes. $8 per box.

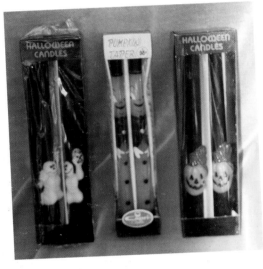

Three packages of taper style candles with figural additions. $12 ea pr.

Three boxes of 10" candles, figural tapers. $12 ea. pr.

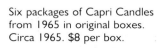

Six packages of Capri Candles from 1965 in original boxes. Circa 1965. $8 per box.

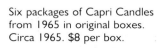

Cat on jack-o'-lantern candle. $4.

Capri Candles box. We finally saw the end of the cartons and cartons of these we had. We sold them for a dollar a box, so they must be worth $3 each, now that we no longer have any left!

Black cat candle. $5.

Witch candle. $8.

Tally Cards, Invitations, and Place Cards

Tally cards, invites, and place cards often overlap or serve dual purposes. Sometimes the same item was printed in more than one way. Regardless, these are small gems, graphic mementos of Halloween. They can be saved in an album, displayed in a case, framed and put on the wall, or placed in small baskets. They may even be used for their original purpose. The Art Deco models tend to demand the most attention because of the fabulous colors, as well as the designs. These objects are very popular both because they are small and because they are still affordable.

Tri fold invite. $12.

Right and far right: A changing place card, open and closed. $12.

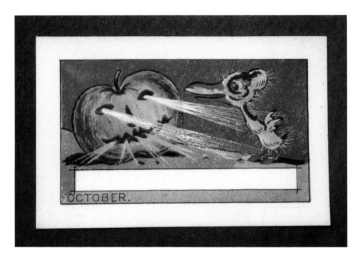

Prang lithographed card from set of the months. $15.

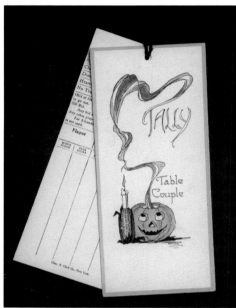

Right and far right: Whist parties were once a popular pastime and these cards were used to keep score. $6 ea.

Trick or Treat Trader covers from the early years were made as postcards, cut out from the back page of the issues, and used as name cards at a party. Circa 1985. $2.

Two place cards. $4.

A card that opens to a three dimensional effect. Showing both sides. $20.

Whitney place card, closed and open with fortune showing. $12.

Beistle made this cute little guy in all sizes, but this one is perfect for a nut cup with a name written on his belly. $7.

Rocker bottom place card. $6.

Two invitations. $6 ea.

Invite to a frolic. $8.

Sweet little card with poem.
$6.

A very deco tally. $12.

Tally up with this rather saucy witch. $6.

Two little invite cards. $6 ea.

Invite card. $6.

Tally card. $6.

Mechanical black cat place card. $15.

Two tally cards. $6 ea.

Two little invite cards. $6 ea.

Tongue Twister, mechanical place card. $10.

Dance cards are passé today, but they once served an important place in society. $8.

A charming Deco place card. $8.

Two die cut place cards. $12 ea.

A sweet little tally card printed in Germany. $8.

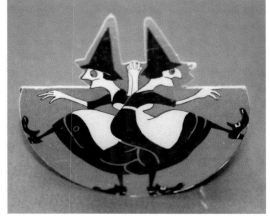

Two little invitations. $6 ea.

Fold up nut cup with a spot for a name. $12.

Rocker type card. $8.

Two charming place cards. $10 ea.

Is this card a subtle hint? $8.

A Deco Greeting. $8.

A die cut advertising card which I couldn't resist adding to this section, just because of size. $20.

J.C. Carter of Boston produced cards for
dances, menus, tallys, etc. $15 ea.

No. 1729 J.C.

No. 1601 J.C.

Two place cards. $6 ea.

Two Tally cards. $6 ea.

A wonderful die cut stand up fortune place marker. $20.

A box set of 5 pumpkin head favors by Beistle. $30.

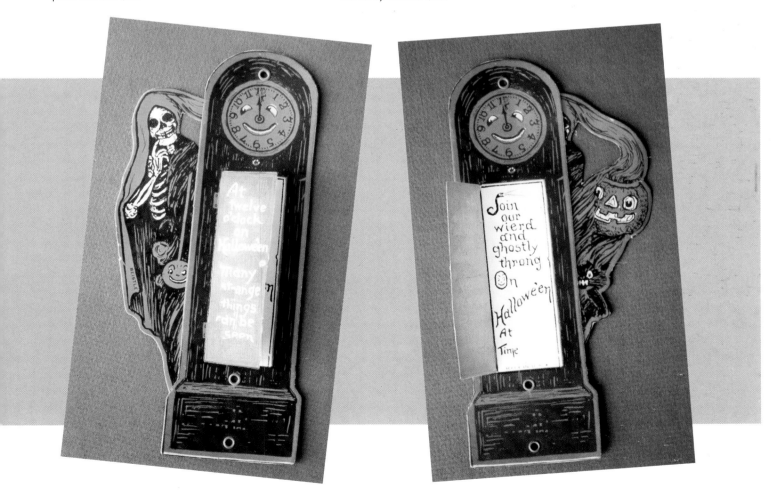

A mechanical invite figure moves from side to side. The clock case door opens as well. $20.

Place card with added nut cup. $12.

Two tally cards with children from artist Ellen Clapsaddle's Wolf period. Clapsaddle is known best for her postcard art with sweet children. $15 ea.

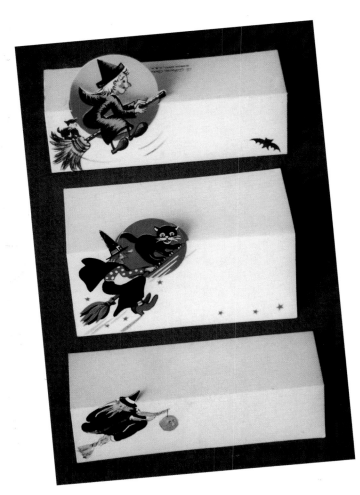

Three place cards with cut out figures to give dimensionality. $8 ea.

Two Tally cards. $8 ea.

Tally card and invite card. $6 ea.

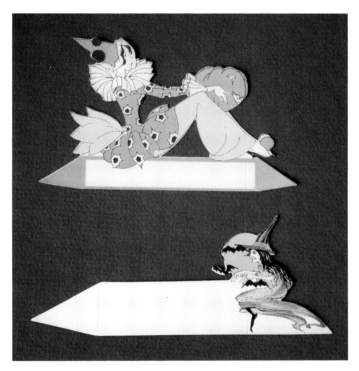

Two place cards: the Art Deco girl is
$10, the witch is $5.

Two Tally cards: witch with moon, $6; witch in
yellow may be a Whitney design, $12.

Do Goblins really Gobble? A
greeting, $5; an invite, $7.

A rather unusual place card with a fortune inside the nut shell when it opens. $12.

A Deco place card, $10, and a neat invite, $12.

I have never been sure why they put items like these on cupcakes, right into the frosting. When I was young, in the school bake sale, there they were. These cardboard figures were always ruining the frosting. $2 ea.

Two place cards. $6 ea.

Complete package of Tally
cards by Taylor. $25.

Invite. $4.

Two little invite cards. $6 ea.

Two tally cards. $6 ea.

Two tally cards. $6 ea.

Closed and open, this little place card is a fun cat item, $8.

Blacky and Spotty stood
on the fence
Yowling, but in playful mien,
Enjoying themselves as
I hope you will
On this merry Hallowe'en.

Two Art Deco place cards. $10 ea.

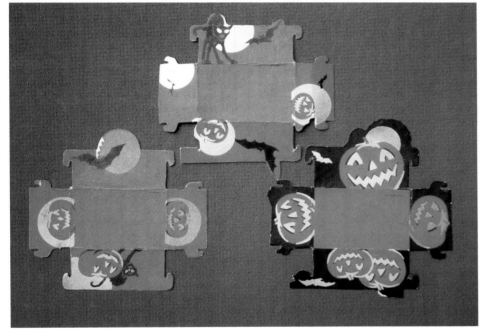

Fold them up and you will have three nut cups. $10 ea.

Stick them in a nut cup, a cupcake or anywhere else you feel needs a festive flare. Jack-o'-lantern man, $8.00. Jack-o'-lantern, $5.

Tally card. $8.

Two rocking bottom place cards. $6 ea.

Two tally cards. $5 ea.

Two charming tally cards. $8 ea.

Two rocker bottom place cards. $6 ea.

Two tallys, the one on the right displays the table numbers someone has written on them. $6 ea.

Two place cards. The witch, $7; the Deco girl, $10.

Two Tally cards. The Scotty dog was a very popular motif and it is not surprising that he just trotted onto the Halloween table as he, like Burns, is a Scot! Scotty, $12; cauldron, $5.

Two tallys, that display the table numbers someone has written on them. $6 ea.

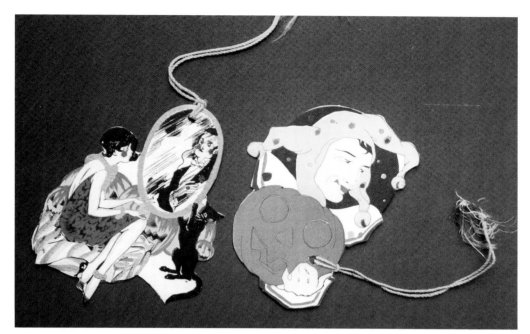

Two Deco tally cards: one showing the tradition of a girl looking into a mirror and seeing her true love. Her red dress has witches for print. Wish I could find material like that! $12. Jester, $10.

Are owls really scary? These children think so. The owl's hoot is breaking up a game of blind mans buff! $12.

Two invites with black cats. $6 ea.

Two place cards. $6 ea.

Top left:
An invitation to stop one in ones tracks. $8.

Top right:
Five place cards. The top two are probably by the popular children's artist Bernhardt Wall. Top row, $10 ea. The rest, $6 ea.

Left:
Two greetings with charms and fortunes on the mind of the sender. $6 ea.

Right:
Ghostly place card and bewitching invite. $6 ea.

Below:
Two place cards. Could the one of the Brownie be a Palmer Cox (an earlier popular children's artist). It has the right look. $14. Cat, $6.

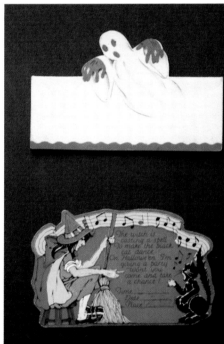

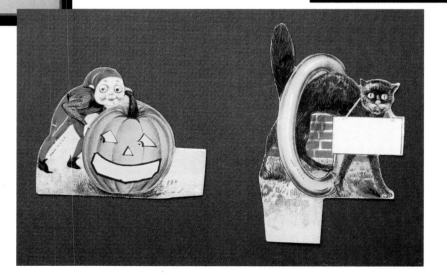

Two place cards: the little boy is by Ellen Clapsaddle, $12; the candle
carrying child is worth $10.

Two place cards: ugly witch, $5; beautiful witch, $10.

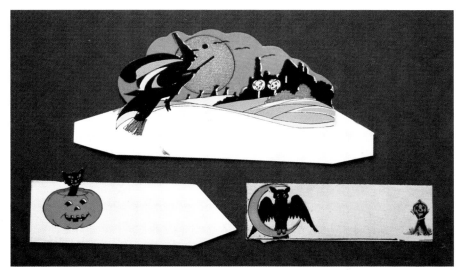

Three place cards: larger Deco card with witch, $6; the other two, $1 ea.

Two place cards. I feel the one with the little people carving the jack-o'-lantern is the essence of fantasy. How I hope these beings are at work in my garden! $8 ea.

Two place cards with diecut figures. $6 ea.

Invite. $6.

Cat with candle place card. $7.

Things That Go on the Table

Here you will find food containers, centerpieces, and everything that was not in the previous subsections (unless they are being saved for future chapters). I have added full pages of the Reed catalogue for c. 1938 as they show many of the items as they were sold by the company. What a joy it is to find a catalogue like this for research.

Three waxed cardboard egg nog cartons. The two Borden's containers are test pieces from the Mid-west. It is hoped that someday Borden will distribute them around the country. Schepps, $20. Borden's, $40 ea.

Three different bags: scarecrow by Funworld, haunted house by Topstone Industries. $1 ea.

What table is complete without a bag like this full of goodies, placed at every setting? It is unfortunate that bags like these have lost popularity in the last few decades. Package, $10.

Package of treat bags. 50 for 29 cents. No maker's mark but made in USA. $15.

Three different bags. $1 ea.

Woman's Home Companion page showing some table decorations. $6.

Ladies' Home Journal, October 1919, sheet showing amongst other things a table fully set. An Elizabeth Bissell "The New Halloween Frolics" page. $6.

Above and left:
Nut cups full of candy or mints or nuts are great to place on the table at each place. $2-8 ea.

A sample label, made in England for hopeful distribution in the States. The Crackers were the type you put as a party favor at each place and one would pull the ends and a bang would go off. Then you would open the favor and inside it would be a prize or a gift of some sort, like a silly hat. To our knowledge, these were never produced and the thirteen sample labels are the only ones known in the printer's archives. $150.

Nut cups or mint baskets made from crepe, cardboard, and paper. $5-12.

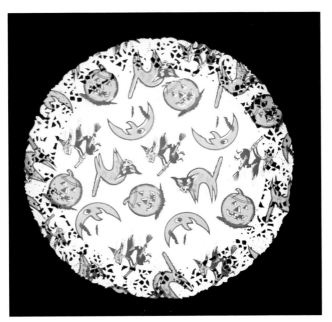

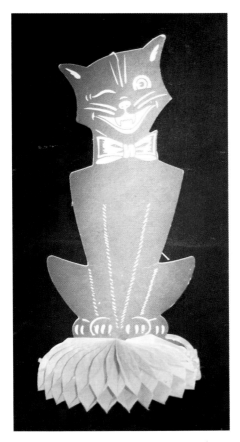

Cardboard cat on an accordion tissue base. A centerpiece which will enhance any table. $25.

Lacy doily that, thankfully, never made it under a cake! *Gift from Rebecca Venable.* $6.

Left and below:
Boxed set of *Children's
Hallowe'en Party Book*. $125.

Though only a few years old, this
set—which is more Autumn than
Halloween—may be used all year
round and is much in demand. The
set was so inexpensive (sold for only
$35), it seems awfully cheap for a
cookie jar, pitcher, and tea set.

I carried these back from England because I felt the bottles were so wonderful! The beer is for sale, I believe, on the West Coast. Fiddler's Elbow, Old Devil and Hobgoblin beer are from Wytchwood Brewery in Whitney, England. The labels are graphically brilliant, the embossed witch on the bottle and the lithographed witch on the cap both enhance the whole look. A fun addition to the table. After they are consumed, you can keep the bottles in your collection. The Brewery is "fiercely independent" and growing in popularity. $6 ea.

Modern teapot made in China of ... china. $7.

A Tiny Golden Book, # 14 in the series and the only Halloween related one. Perfect as a stuffer in a candy bag on a nut cup. $12.

Two party favors to fancy up the table. Crepe dressed doll, $12. Favor, $5.

Little hats were placed on the table with persons name underneath and guests would have to look and choose until they found their place. $5.

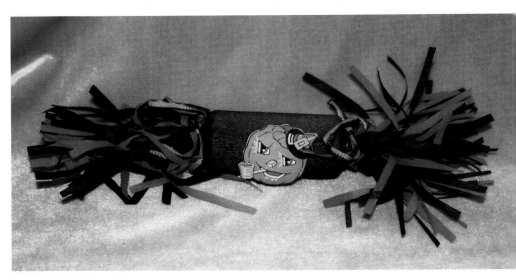

Party favor, cracker. $12.

Milk for your coffee or tea, in a 1997
Broguiere's Dairy Bottle. $7.

John Ottman's (composer of the music from *Halloween H20,*) *Portrait of Terror* CD is using
photos from our two previous Halloween books as background for the cover and the disc.
VSD-5986. 1998 Miramax Film Corp. The music is perfect for Halloween mood music. $18.

How can one sit at a table and eat without music? *Walt Disney's
Trick or Treat Stories and Songs of Halloween*. $15.

Phantom Phavorites CD is a jack-o'-lantern face! $10.

Above and right:
Halloween lollipop holders. The lollipop would be the face. $75 for Hattie, $65 for Harry and Tom. Owl, $15. These holders are considered to be in mint condition as they are shown.

Fold together and, voila, you have a nut cup. $14.

A lovely table setting for Halloween. Booklet, $12.

Page from a 1958, #558 Dennison Party book *Let's have a Party* (cost 50 cents), showing a table decorated for Halloween. $15.

Nut cup. $8.

Clever Idea Party Makers original package of 8 nut cups for 29 cents. $22.

Crepe border for around the table or as a strip down the center of a plain table cover. Complete roll, $10.

Pages 136 to 139 show some of the pages from the C.A. Reed Co. catalogue from 1938. From here you can see the products set out in the original catalogue as they would have been offered for sale to the stores. The entire catalogue, $150.

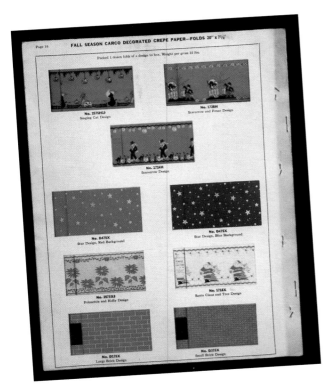

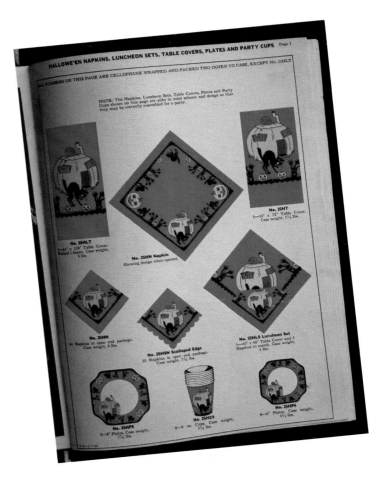

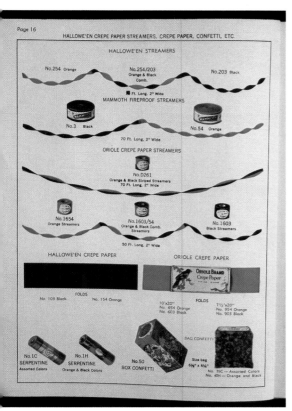

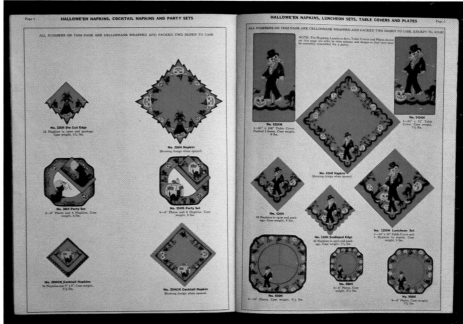

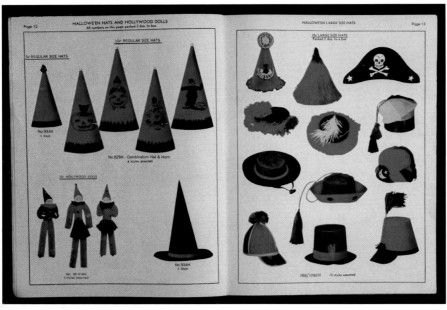

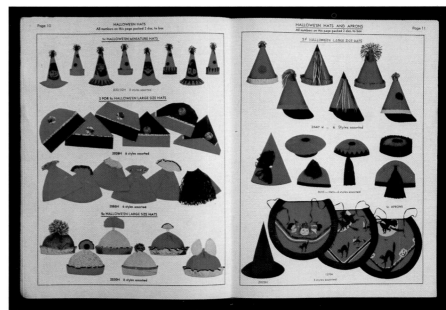

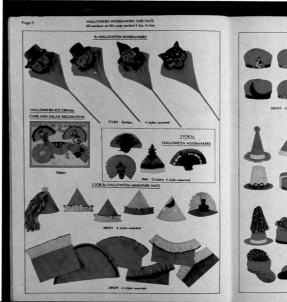

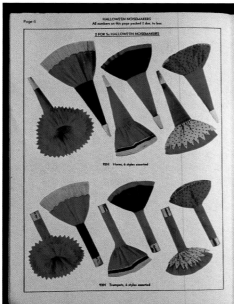

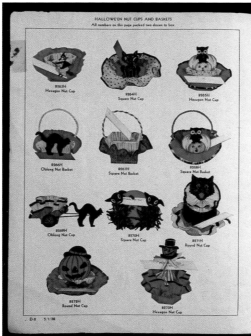

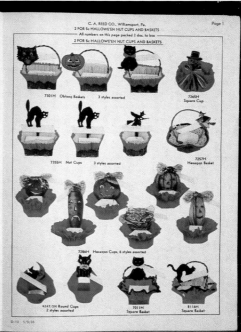

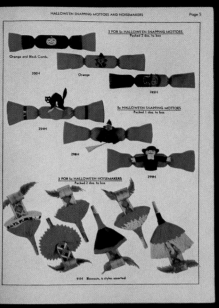

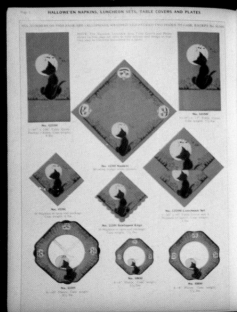

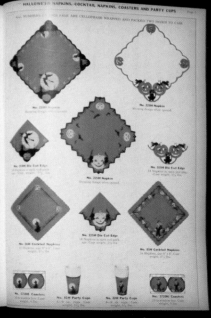

Halloween Frolic is a song book full of Hallow-een music to be sung at parties. 1908. $45.

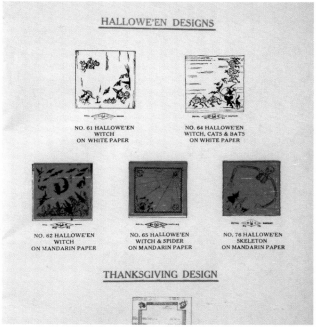

Half page from 1927 American Tissue Mills catalogue. Complete catalogue, $45.

So where is the box? The Johnston's chocolates tag was memorable enough for someone to keep as a momento. Wish my cat could play a fiddle like that! $10.

Folk Art, Insider Art, Modern Artists and Crafts People

There is an incredible revival of folk art and artist-created Halloween ornamentation underway. Lanterns, paintings, luminaries, figures, ornaments, and other objects are popping full grown out of the world of fantasy into our lives. There are some extremely talented people making this possible. In this chapter are just a few of the many artists who are making today's Halloween so exciting. Salvador Dali, the Surrealist, would have loved some of this stuff! Who knows, years from now some of these artists may be in museums. In fact, some already are!

Age has nothing to do with merit and the items we have chosen for this chapter are just a tenth of the ones we should have liked to include. The Southern face jugs are included because they are wonderful examples of peripheral Halloween folk art. Imagine meeting one of these guys on Halloween night!

Fantasy is a very broad, and constantly expanding, genre. Everyone's fantasies are different because everyone's desires, fears, senses of humor, and concepts of beauty are different. We are fortunate that creativity is again being focused on Halloween and that the items are so affordable as vintage items of the same caliber are so much more expensive. As with other chapters, the old, the new and the in-between are included.

Remember, folk art is produced by self trained artists while crafts are made by people who follow instructions on how to do something some one else has already done. Reproductions are exact copies, or close to, of items already made and are made to take the place of the originals. Fakes are reproductions passed off as originals. An original is a joy to own. Reproductions are to be used and not collected.

This hand painted silk lampshade was painted in 1998 by Rebecca Venable of the Cobweb. Notice the Ouija board and the intricate details in the witches hat. This piece is a one of a kind item. $400.

A nice composition candle holder designed by Marie Cubero-Moretz of the Cross Creek Collection. $20.

Halloween pins on cards by Marie Cubero-Moretz of Cross Creek Collection. $10 ea.

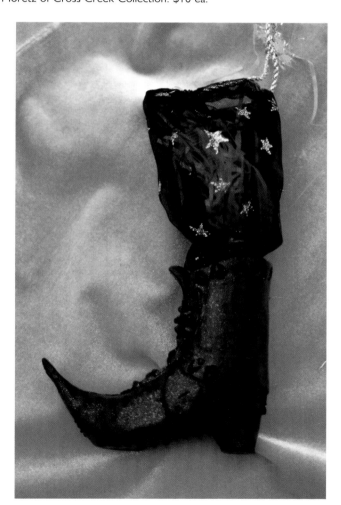

This jack-o'-lantern with paper backed eyes and ivy covered bail in heavy composition was designed by Marie Cubero-Moretz of the Cross Creek Collection. $25.

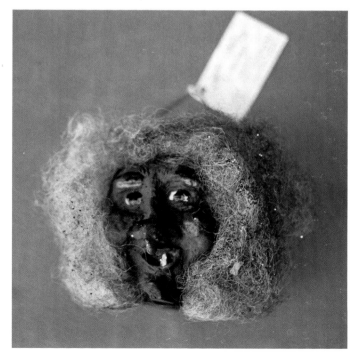

This charming piece can be used all year long as an old fashioned shoe candy container with orange paper shreds inside. Designed by Marie Cubero-Moretz of Cross Creek Collection. $15.

A witches cauldron with witches face and fuzzy hair by Marie Cubero-Moretz of the Cross Creek Collection. $25.

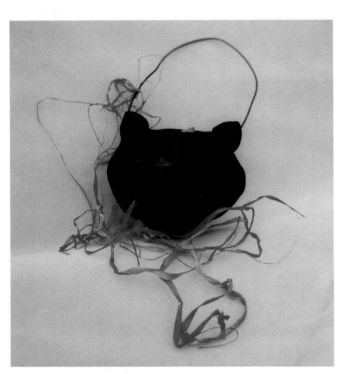

A fanciful candy container of a jack-o'-lantern boy by Marie Cubero-Moretz. $40.

Cat lantern with paper grass, which looks lovely behind the cut out features. $20.

This two piece carved paper mache witch box is an awesome piece indeed. By Rick Conant. $125.

Rick Conant hand cuts the faces on his designs. Originally an actor, he made a few items for himself. Soon everyone wanted them. Now he has little time to act because his artwork is a full time job. This carved, paper mache spice box (complete with spice containers) has a paper backed face. $125.

A two piece carved Top Hat Jack-O'-Lantern box which gives new meaning to the word stove pipe hat! Paper mache sculptured box by Rick Conant. $80.

A seven piece Halloween totem of carved paper mache and paper backed faces, by Rick Conant. $350.

Small round Trick or Treat paper mache box by Rick Conant. $35.

A carved paper mache box called Bat and Full Moon. Part of three piece set, the other two are not shown. By Rick Conant. $50 ea.

Five oval boxes made of carved paper mache and backed with paper. Rick Conant. $225.

Four carved wood lanterns faces backed with paper. $28 ea.

Virginia Betourne, of Trout Creek American Folk Art, designs and creates each piece individually. Paper mache pomegranate man holding a cat noise maker and wearing a Halloween hat on his jack-o'-lantern head. $80.

Southern folk art devil jug by Flowers. Nicely glazed with sweat puddles of blue, inset teeth, and bulging eyes. $150.

Onion Goblin holding a postcard and sitting on a jack-o'-lantern. Original tag. From Trout Creek American Folk Art, by Virginia Betourne. $125.

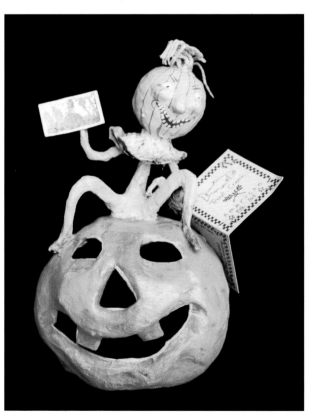

Left:
This wonderful piece of fantasy with a cabbage leaf body is a trick or treater I dearly would love to have come ring my door bell. How about you? A Trout Creek, Virginia Betourne original. $125.

A lovely green glaze on this Southern folk art jug by Carl Lockman. $155.

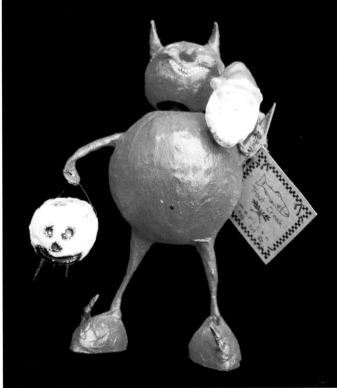

The Devil and Santa go trick or treating disguised as each other. Nodder heads. Santa carries a devil mask and the devil carries a Santa mask. Trout Creek, Virginia Betourne originals. $90 ea.

Left and below:
Old sap buckets cut with Halloween designs to be used as luminaries. $12 ea.

Below:
This is a very unusual Southern folk art piece by Flowers. It is not only a jug but a hanging wall sconce! The tongue has a red glaze on it, and it is so Krampus like! Krampus or Grampus is the hairy devil like creature who, in Austria, goes around with Santa Claus and beats up the bad people. He has a long tongue and carries a switch. He is scary and the celebrations in Austria are, I understand, rather hairy! $250

Marie Rogers folk art jug with scary inset teeth. I should not like to meet this guy under any circumstance! Much too scary. $250.

Day of the Dead skull by Rebecca Venable. $35.

Early tin tray, painted in 1997 by John Moreno. The house in the background is where I live and Jack and Sally are being married in our yard! This is a one of a kind item. $250.

Early tin tray decorated with scene from *Nightmare Before Christmas*, the Disney-Burton movie. One of a kind, painted by John Moreno in 1997. $250.

Ratchet noise makers of Jack and Sally, by Rebecca Venable. There were only a handful of these made for Christmas presents in 1998. $75 pr.

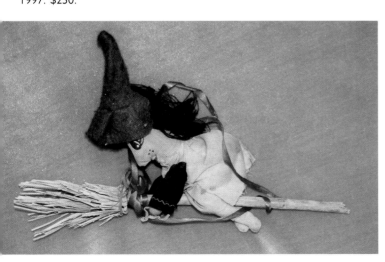

Bruja made by the Indians of Venezuela. Gift from one witch doctor to another. $20.

Early cut metal figure of witch and cat. Artist unknown. $250.

Devil candy container of composition, crepe and cardboard. Rebecca Venable. $55.

Jack-o'-lantern headed scare crow candy container of composition, cardboard, and crepe by Rebecca Venable. $55.

Jack Skelington from *Nightmare Before Christmas*. Wood and pipe cleaner figures made for friends as Christmas gifts by Rebecca Venable of the Cob Web. $10 ea.

Painted gourd basket by Rebecca Venable. $35.

A modern aged cut steel figure of a witch. Artist unknown. $30.

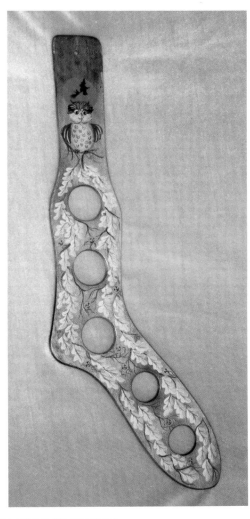

Old wooden sock form decorated by S. Thompson in 1984. $35.

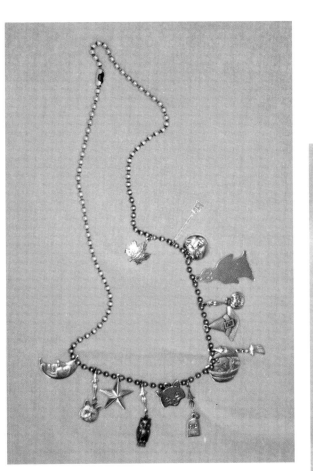

Charm necklace made by Rebecca Venable. $45.

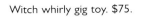

Witch whirly gig toy. $75.

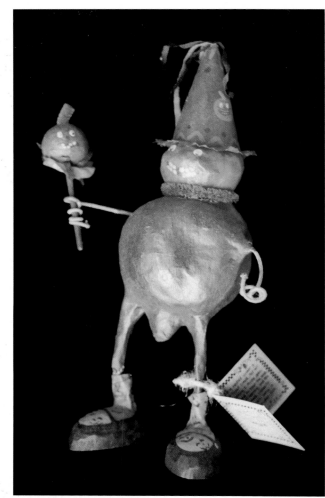

Pomegranate Man holding a jack-o'-lantern noise maker by Virginia Betourne of Trout Creek. $80.

Laughing Onion Goblin with carrot and cat lantern by Virginia Betourne of Trout Creek. $125.

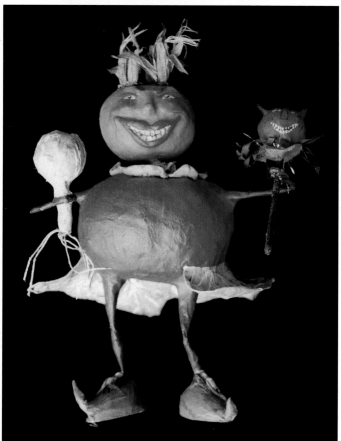

This "Corn Goddess" is the voluptuous spirit of the earth. Ginny designed her for me and now she waits, with her inscrutable smile, for her mate that will arrive soon. Created by Virginia Betourne of Trout Creek. $150.

Cat lantern necklace by Virginia
Betourne of Trout Creek. $30.

From turn of the century oak organ pipes, John Moreno
created a wonderful venue for the *Nightmare Before
Christmas* characters. Only two sets were made. $2800.

Trout Creek pin of anthropomorphic veggies by
Virginia Betourne. $20 ea.

Boots scraper cast iron in original
green paint, ca. 1920-30. $250.

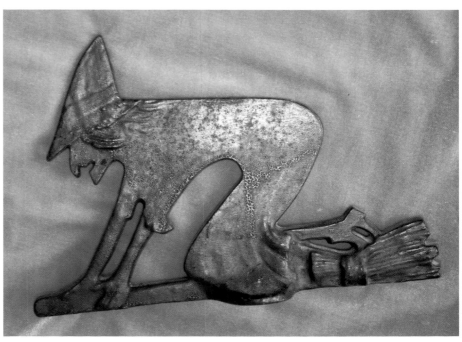

A lovely pumpkin colored handkerchief crocheted and stenciled Halloween 1997. Made by Mary Dewey as a gift for friends. $10.

Two noise makers: cat and jack-o'-lantern man, artist signed. $45 ea.

Two dancing figures by Rebecca Venable. $15 ea.

S. Thompson, old wooden spoon, 1987 decoration. $12.

Above and right:
John Moreno painted these two large signs for my shop. I think they are wonderful. $300 ea.

Two postcards of paintings by surrealist artist Kathy Staico Schorr. The cards were made of her paintings, which were in an exhibition in 1997, "Strange Things Are Seen." Oil on canvas, 24" x 30", is jack-o'-lanterns and trick or treaters in true "Daliistic" tradition. $3000 painting; postcards, $5 ea.

Kathy Stacio Schorr is a professional artist whose paintings are often exhibited and sold in galleries. Painting on canvas. $3000.

A fancy picture frame made by Mike Drake of Drake Enterprises. The spooky picture in the frame is a 3D image of Mike and Pumpkinhead from the movie of the same name. $45.

This incredible jack-o'-lantern man, with all his lanterns, personifies the earthiness and zanyness of Halloween. Even the clothing is sewn together in patches. This was created by Jack Rhodes, a retired art teacher. The big noses are a character trait of his work. $400.

The Games, Fortunes, Fun, and Forfeits of Halloween

Halloween is a social time and game playing is a very important part of the holiday, especially if the games are scary or can predict the future. In Robert Burn's poem "Halloween," he tells of fortunes by the fire. Predicting the future—especially with regards to who one would marry, and when and how happy and prosperous that marriage was to be—made fortune telling games of great importance to the participants.

This category is really a catch all for collectors who collect games and fortune telling related items. As fortune telling is as old as the pyramids of Egypt and has always been a popular and important social part of Halloween, it deserves to be delved into from all directions. Tarot decks, Ouija boards, and forfeit games have always been very popular. Movies and tall tales have given the Ouija board a diabolic persona, which is quite undeserved. Myth and reality are very easily confused. Whether you collect games for use or because they are interesting and decorative is strictly up to the collector. Board games used for decorating walls can be very appealing and new age. Those who are uncomfortable with such items are recommended to not use, collect, or own them. There are many collectors quite happy to add them to their collections.

The Spinning Witch, 1921, by R. Peck DeSnoyers. $65.

Punch boards were once a popular game for forfeits and sometimes money was charged. $15 ea.

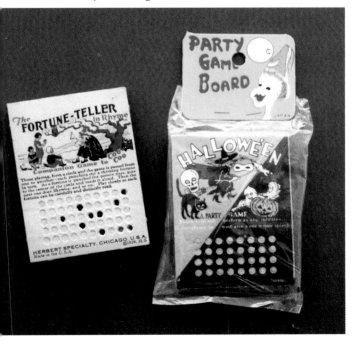

Crystal balls, 8 balls, casting of the bones and roasting the chestnuts are just some of the fun games of Halloweens past, games that are collected and enjoyed by all generations. Some collectors refer to these items as vintage New Age collectibles! Graphically, these games are often very colorful, except for the Fuld boards, which are a bit bleak and barren of color.

Crystal Balls are perhaps the most mystical of all the items that are used at Halloween, or depicted on Halloween items. Halloween is fun and all of these games and activities enhance it as well as add mystery to the night. Looking into my Crystal Ball! I see you having a grand time this Halloween!

Hallowe'en Kitty Card Game. $45.

Three out of a set of six postcards by cat artist Louis Wain. $65 ea.

Ouija Queen board by American Novelty
Company. *Collection of Elayne Star.* $30.

Planchette Polka sheet music from 1868, composed by Aug. La
Motte. *From the Collection of Elayne Star.* $20.

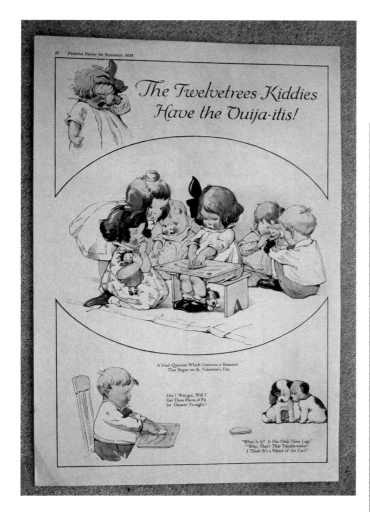

Above and right:
Pictorial Review, 1920, two page comic drawing for children by artist
C.H. Twelvetrees. *From the Elayne Star Collection.* $15.

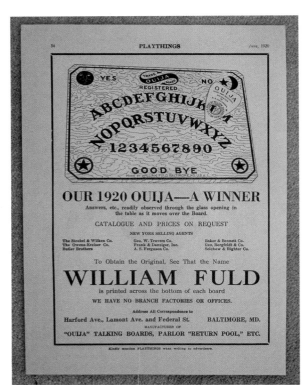

Soul Link, a Ouija type board of solid wood, handmade and artist signed on reverse by Ken Handy. *From the Elayne Star Collection.* $40.

Advertising page from *Playthings Magazine*, advertising the 1920 Ouija. William Fuld was the owner and producer of the Ouija board and made it a popular toy. *From the Elayne Star Collection.* $5.

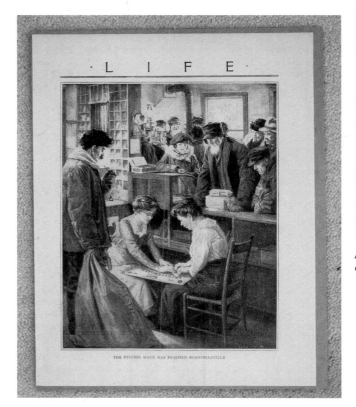

A wooden Witchboard with planchet by Caer Lloer Dyn Products, handmade, contemporary Canadian board. *From the Elayne Star Collection.* $35.

April 29, 1920 *Life* magazine page showing the enjoyment people received watching players, and playing with, the Ouija. *From the Elayne Star Collection.* $15.

This green eyed Ouija type board has got to be the funkiest of all boards. Made by Transogram Canada Ltd. in 1967, it glows in the dark. *Contemporary. From the Elayne Star Collection.* $65.00.

Angel Board by Angel Alliance Network, Inc. 1996. This Ouija type board is made of cardboard with a plastic planchet to help you communicate with angels. *From the Elayne Star Collection.* $40.

Angel Guidance Board, 1995, by J&J Inspirations. This board, with a circular planchet, is popular with collectors and users who feel that angels guard and guide the users of the board. *From the Elayne Star Collection.* $25.

Mystic Heart by Relationship Enrichment Systems, 1993. A cardboard board, Ouija type game. Notice the heart shaped planchet. *From the Elayne Star Collection.* $30.00

Clear Channel Board by The Channel Board Co. 1991.
From the Elayne Star Collection. $35.

Magic Marvel, The Wonder Answer Board by
Lee Industries, 1944. This game has to have
one of the most colorful of all the boards. *From
the Elayne Star Collection.* $35.

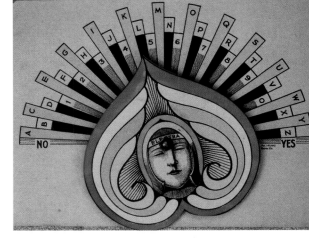

Right:
Electa Co. made one of
the most beautiful of all
the Ouija types with a
very Art Nouveau style
planchette. Circa 1910.
*From the Elayne Star
Collection.* $125.

Genii, The Witches' Fortune Teller by Milton Bradley. Though the
box is almost gone, the label is still intact and that is a real bonus for
any collector. 1896. *From the Elayne Star Collection.* $125.

Round Talking Board with planchet, 1997 by Third Eye
Concepts. *From the Elayne Star Collection.* $35.

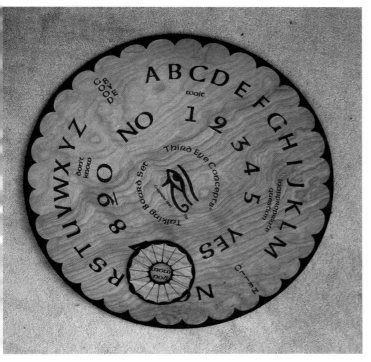

Third Eye Concepts Talking Board Set, 1991.
From the Elayne Star Collection. $30.

Third Eye Concepts Talking Board, 1997. *From the Elayne Star Collection.* $25.

Videos from *Witchboard I* and *II* . *Witchboard I*, 1986 by Paragon Arts Int. Prod, starring Tod Allen, Tawny Kitaeen, and Steph Nichols. Written and directed by Kevin Tenney. *Witchboard II* stared Ami Dolez, Timothy Gibbs, John Gatins, and Laraine Newman. A 1993 Republic Picture. Two movies about everything the Ouija is believed by many to be, but isn't. You won't really want to watch these more than once. *From the Elayne Star Collection.* $10 ea.

The Amazing Answer Board glows in the dark. Yogee is another take off of the Ouija name. Lee Industries, 1944. *From the Elayne Star Collection.* $40.

Left and below:
Midas Golden Touch & Prophesying Board. 1987.
From the Elayne Star Collection. Canadian $20 box
and game.

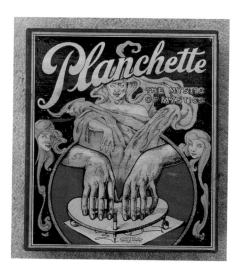

Planchet, The Mystic of Mystics by Selchow
& Righter Co. First made in 1860. *From the
Elayne Star Collection.* $75.

Planchette Talking Board, F.H. Ayres,
Ltd., London. (The box is marked A.W.
Gamage. Ltd.) *From the Elayne Star
Collection.* $75.

The original Planchette dates back to the time of Pythagoras, ca. 540 BC. Planchette, two different versions. *From the Elayne Star Collection.* $75 ea.

Weyers Bros. Scientific Instrument Makers of London made this Planchette. *From the Elayne Star Collection.* $75.

Two William Fuld Ouija planchettes from the 1915 era with a boxed Fuld Egyptian Luck Board. *From the Elayne Star Collection.* $40 ea.

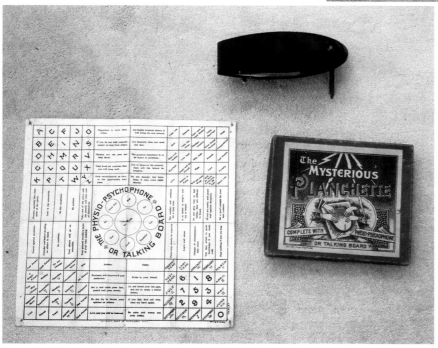

The Mysterious Planchette, made in England. *From the Elayne Star Collection.* $75.

Mystifying Oracle by William Fuld. Pat. No. 56,001, board and planchet. *From the Elayne Star Collection.* $20.

Ouija by William Fuld with original box. 1919. *From the Elayne Star Collection.* $15.

Ouija Board by William Fuld, plywood board, 1920. *From the Elayne Star Collection.* $20.

Ouija The Mystifying Oracle
Wonderful Talking Board box.
Copyright 1919. *From the Elayne
Star Collection.* $20.

Two wonderful miniature Ouija boards with planchettes.
Barbara Hall Miniatures, 1997 and Diane Vasco Miniatures, 1987. *From the Elayne Star Collection.* $5 ea.

Ouija by William Fuld, 1950s. *From the Elayne
Star Collection.* $20.

Mystifying Oracle Ouija by William Fuld, ca.
1920s. *From the Elayne Star Collection.* $25.

Ouija Mystifying Oracle William Fuld Talking Board Set by Parker Bros. Parker Bros. bought out Fuld, who was the guru and populizer of the Ouija, ca. 1972. *From the Elayne Star Collection.* $8.

Ouija Board from Baltimore Talking Board Co.,1920. *From the Elayne Star Collection.* $35.

Mystical ESP Board by Olympia Educational Game Co. *From the Elyane Star Collection.* $30.

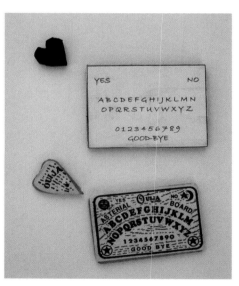

Two miniature boards with their planchettes. Chelsea Beater, 1998, & Shackman. *From the Elayne Star Collection.* $5 ea.

Left:
Miniature Ouija board by Smidgens, 1998. Planchette in original box. *From the Elayne Star Collection.* $4.

Right:
Miniature Ouija board with planchet. *From the Elayne Star Collection.* $10.

Hasko Mystic Board by Haskelite, ca. 1940s. *From the Elayne Star Collection.* $20.

Espirito, early wooden board, double sided, maple veneer on plywood. *From the Elayne Star Collection.* $50.

Early double sided wooden (maple veneer on plywood) Ouija Board (probably a William Fuld board). *From the Elayne Star Collection.* $50.

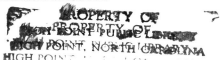

Early wooden Ouija with planchet. *From the Elayne Star Collection.* $50.

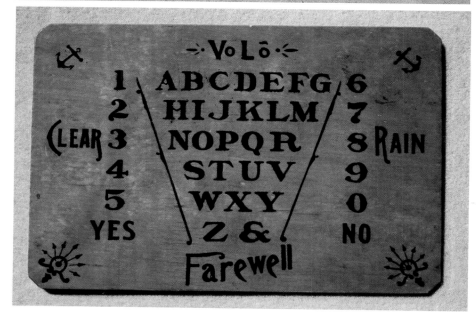

VoLo early wooden board. Possibly a William Fuld. *From the Elayne Star Collection.* $35.

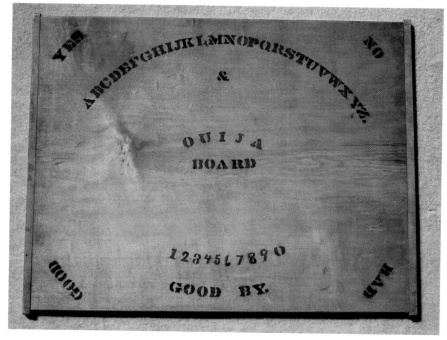

Early Ouija board, hand painted and stenciled on a 1/2" wooden bread board. This game has a Parcheesi board on the reverse. Notice the word "bye" is spelled wrong. *From the Elayne Star Collection.* $50.

Early wooden Ouija, J.M. Simmons & Co., 1919. *From the Elayne Star Collection.* $35.

Ouija by Morton E. Converse & Son Co. An early wooden board with planchet. *From the Elayne Star Collection.* $25.

The Mitche Manitou Board by Wilder Mfg. 1920. *From the Elyane Star Collection.* $35.

Oriole wooden board and planchette by the Issac Fuld Southern Toy Co., ca. 1905. *From the Elayne Star Collection.* $60.

Swami The Talking Board by Cardinal Industries. *From the Elayne Star Collection.* $30.

A talking board made for the Spanish speaking market. *From the Elayne Star Collection.* $35.

Very early dark wooden board. *From the Elayne Star Collection.* $20.

Ouija Queen with matching planchet by American Novelty Co. *From the Elayne Star Collection.* $40.

Mystic Answer Board by Remington Morse, 1944. *From the Elayne Star Collection.* $22.

Cardboard Ouija type game, Magi-Board. Psychic-Graf, Inc. 1943. *From the Elayne Star Collection.* $25.

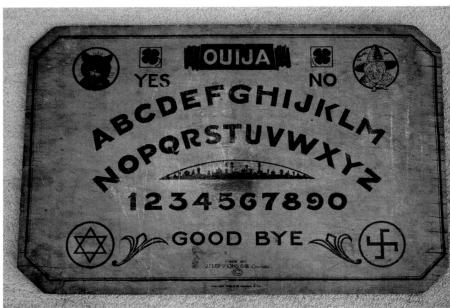

Ouija board by J.M. Simmons Co., 1919. *From the Elayne Star Collection.* $30.

Advertisement. Page from *Playthings Magazine,* June 1920. *From the Elayne Star Collection.* $8.

Ouija by Craftsman Sales Co. *From the Elayne Star Collection.* $25.

The Mysterious Planchet by the Planchet Co. *From the Elayne Star Collection.* $45.

Zolar's Mystic Genii Board by Zolar Enterprises Inc., 1965. *From the Elayne Star Collection.* $30.

Witchboard, ca.1987, has a warning on it not to play alone. From the movie *Witchboard,* which opened on Friday the 13th. The warning should have been not to watch the movie alone or you would be bored to tears by the slapstick sensationalism. *From the Elayne Star Collection.* $20.

Swami Mystery Talking Board by Gift Craft, ca. 1940. *From the Elayne Star Collection.* $22.

Early wooden board with a pine planchet, 1891, by Kennard Novelty Co. *From the Elayne Star Collection.* $65.

The Ouija Board, Magic Box, 1995, Random House distribution. *From the Elayne Star Collection.* $25.

The Angels Talk, by Penguin Studio, 1997. A cardboard game with planchet. Converse with the angels! *From the Elayne Star Collection.* $24.

Mystery Talking Board by E.S. Lowe Co.
Masonite board. *From the Elayne Star Collection.*
$30.

Mystic Soothsayer by Drueke. Wooden board.
From the Elayne Star Collection. $35.

Black (African) Magic Talking Board by Gift Craft.
Fiberboard. *From the Elayne Star Collection.* $35.

The Sphinx Speaks. Masonite. *From the Elayne Star Collection.* $35.

The Wireless Messenger by the Wm. W. Wheeler Co. Wooden tray and planchette. *From the Elayne Star Collection.* $75.

The Psychograph, an early talking board. *From the Elayne Star Collection.* $125.

The Magical Wizard Talking Board with planchette by Fortune Industries. *From the Elayne Star Collection.* $25.

Haskelite Manufacturing produced this Mystic Tray, ca. 1940s game. *From the Elayne Star Collection.* $25.

Pictorial Review magazine cover by children's artist Twelvetrees, October 1920. $12.

Above left:
Haskelite Manufacturing's Hasko Mystic Board, a 1940s game. *From the Elayne Star Collection.* $25.

Mystic Board by Haskelite Manufacturing. *From the Elayne Star Collection.* $35.

Weegee Weegee Tell Me Do sheet music composed by Harry Von Tilzer, the master of novelty tunes using lyrics by William Jerome. 1920. $15.

Ouija Mine sheet music by Willy White with lyrics by Sam Lewis and Joe Young. 1920. Cover by artist Barbelle. $20.

Sheet music, Just A Little Closer, song from a talkie called Remote Control, sung by Lilliam Haines, music by Joseph Meyer. Is there any difference in the magic of electricity in wires, talking words and music hundreds of miles away, and messages through a Ouija coming from another dimension? From the Elyane Star Collection. $12.

Norman Rockwell cover from the Saturday Evening Post of a man and woman playing the Ouija board. May 1920. From the Elyane Star Collection. $12.

Veda The Magic Answer Man, Wiz Novelty Co.,
1920. *From the Elayne Star Collection.* $30.

Ouijas Master postcard. $15.

Above and right:
American Manufacturing
Concern made this Voodoo
table. The bottom of the table
is shown as the instructions
are on the bottom (not
because I thought you'd enjoy
seeing the bottom of a 1939
cardboard table with wooden
frame and legs). $125.

Ouija mouse pad, 1998. $12.

This, above any picture I have ever seen, shows the absorption of society in the table tapping, spirit raising seances. The title "Witchcraft in 1871" from *The Graphic*, Sat Dec. 1871. The caption reads: "Glendover — I can call spirits from the vasty deep. Hotspur — Why so can I, or so can any man; but will they come when you do call for them? Henry the IV part 1 act 3 scene 1." $50.

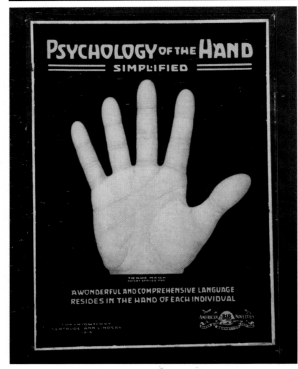

The Crystal Gazer by Parker Bros. is one of the many games that entertained people before the advent of television. *From the Elayne Star Collection.* $150.

Psychology of the Hand. Palm reading and character interpretation from reading the lines— or lack thereof—to determine a persons character and future. This game was copyrighted in 1919 by Gestured Ann Lindsay and produced by American Novelties. $50.

Romany. The people referred to often as Gypsy are the Romany. In the Near and Middle East they are also call Tsigannes. Parker Bros. produced this game in 1898. It was quite common for young ladies to visit the gypsies to find out if they would marry, to whom, and when. $175.

Cards of Fate by J.H. Singer of New York was not
as diabolical as the cover depicted. $95.

Three punch out games. Fortune games were
popular. The Fortune Teller In Rhyme was done in
1929. It is amazing these survived at all as, after all
the punches had been made, players would have
thrown them away. $20 ea.

Coo Coo Fortune Teller punchboard with
original box by Herbert Specialty Mfg. $45.

Consult Elcaro 1914 boxed game. Elcaro is
Oracle spelt backwards. *From the Elayne Star
Collection.* $75.

Finger of Fate game with original box. *From the Elayne Star Collection.* $25.

The Parker Bros. 1897 Black Cat Fortune Telling Game is a favorite of many because of the motif. Parker Bros. Salem, Mass. *From the Elayne Star Collection.* $80.

Madame Zora Fortune Teller Game by Garnell Co., 1935. *From the Elayne Star Collection.* $25.

Witch-ee cover and content by Selchow & Righter Co. *From the Elayne Star Collection.* $45.

Top left:
The Fortune Teller by Pressman Toy Co., NJ., 1989 boxed game. *From the Elayne Star Collection.* $25.

Left:
The Gypsy Fortune Teller by the Milton Bradley Co. *From the Elayne Star Collection.* $80.

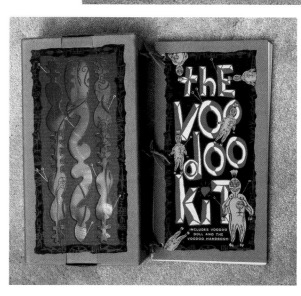

Left:
The Voodoo Kit boxed doll and book set. Running Press Book, 1997. *From the Elayne Star Collection.* $12.

Right:
Eastern Fortune Telling Game by McLaughlin Bros. *From the Elayne Star Collection.* $65.

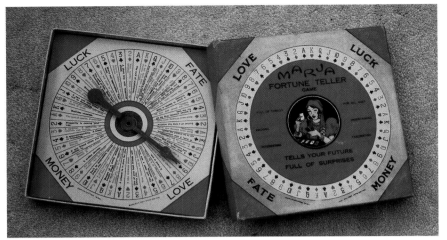

Maraca Fortune Teller Game. Bar-Zim Toy Mfg. Co. 1930. *From the Elayne Star Collection.* $45.

Madame Le Normand's Mystic Cards of Fortune. Merrimack Publishing. *From the Elayne Star Collection.* $25.

Madame Boskey's Fortune Telling Kit by Chronicle Books. *From the Elayne Star Collection.* $12.

The Original Fortune Telling Board Game and box. 1996. *From the Elayne Star Collection.* $30.

The 1979 Mego Co. Fickle Finger of Fate fortune telling game. *From the Elayne Star Collection.* $22.

The Psychic Circle, Sun Anel Innovations, 1995.
Later cardboard boards are often more colorful
than earlier wooden boards. *From the Elayne Star
Collection.* $25.

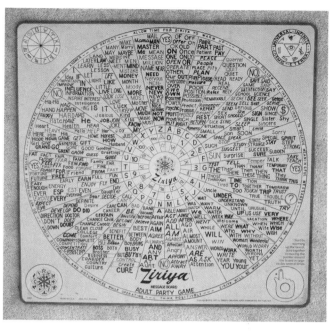

Ziriya Adult Party Game, 1972, Ziriya
Creative Arts Associates. *From the
Elayne Star Collection.* $45.

Ask Zandar box with talking Zandar, by
Milton Bradley. 1992. *From the Elayne
Star Collection.* $30.

Prediction Rod. Parker Bros. 1970. *From the
Elayne Star Collection.* $15.

The Mystiscope Fortune Teller, boxed book with game beside it. 1925. *From the Elayne Star Collection.* $75.

Tin spinner fortune top. *From the Elayne Star Collection.* $35.

An advertising give away or premium from Thom McAn Shoes For Boys. *From the Elayne Star Collection.* $35.

With the toss of the dice, the future is foretold! A 3, 1, and 5 combination, according to this postcard, means "Good luck in business and love affairs." $4.

All the World Fortune Teller by Great Aim Society. *From the Elayne Star Collection.* $45.

The fortune wheel shown on this card has an interesting caption, "Tonight, if you are asked to go walking with a gentleman, Say NO." $8.

Three variations of a fortune wheel game on a postcard. $12 ea.

La Voyante, another fortune wheel game found on a postcard. $20.

In order to play this game you had to cut the card up. Not only did most examples survive intact, but a large store stock was found. $5 ea.

Modern "Fortune Heart," a Valentine's Day novelty. $8.

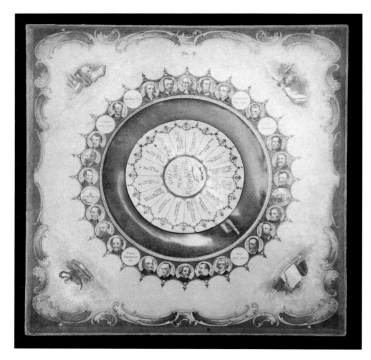

McLaughlin Brothers made Chiromagica, a sort of a history-presidential game. $175.

Milton Bradley Company's Mystic Fortune Teller. $85.

A marvelous 1888 mechanical trade card given to advertise the Columbus Buggy from Columbus, Ohio. "Red hair and White horses are chestnuts, Columbus Buggy Co buggies and happy livery men are facts." Don't you wish you had a fortune like that? These are ephemeral little paper games that seldom survived being played with. $40.

The Eight Ball was shaken, you asked a question, and you learnt the answer. $15.

Fairy Fortune Telling. $145.

Right and center right:
Edward Gorey wrote and designed this tarot terror deck, with corresponding booklet. This is unlike any other tarot deck ever, as it begins by throwing the entire deck into the air to fall disastrously all over the room. This is Gothic humor at its Gorey-est best. Doom, disaster, horrors and more horrors. Brilliant and hilarious. Done for the Gotham Book Mart. This is more fun than any other tarot deck I have ever used or played with! $75, first limited edition (has been reprinted).

US Playing Cards produced
this fortune telling deck. $50.

The Nile Fortune Cards, 1907, US
Playing Card Co. $40.

"Fortune Telling Playing Cards," 1903, Whitman Publishing.
Notice the American Indian swastika symbol of good fortune.
This symbol should never be confused with its reversed coun-
terpart, the Nazi perversion. $60.

Zolar's Astrological Fortune Telling
Horoscope Cards. $25.

The Oracle of Isis deck is based on the Aztec zodiac. An interesting mix as Isis is an Egyptian Goddess while the Aztecs are
from Mexico. 1926, H.P.B. Publishers Inc. $30.

Fortune Telling, An All Fair
Game. $50.

The Halloween Tarot Deck is modern, by
artistically zany and fun U.S. Games Systems.
$30 set.

Prof. A. F. Seward's Fortune Telling
Cards. *From the Elayne Star Collection.* $20.

An interesting vision of Tarot personages with
Tarot cards. $25.

The James Bond 007 Tarot Deck was
designed by Fergus Hall, 1973, Eon
Productions. $50.

U.S. Games System's modern Tarot of the Witches is an artistically done taro. $35.

Carreras Ltd. produced this lovely fortune telling deck. $75.

Posthumous Salvador Dali Tarot Deck by the Guru of Surrealism, late 1980s. $100.

A complete set of advertising tobacco fortune cards, usually found individually from ephemera dealers. $5 ea.

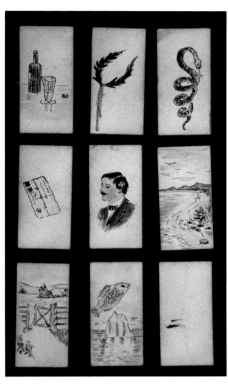

A marvelous hand made Victorian fortune telling deck.
From the Linda Witherill Collection. $250.

Below and right:
Astral Tarot, 1969, Mont-Saint-Johns. $30.

Arthur Gill was one of the comic artists that worked for Tuck. "An Awful Prophecy. Seer: 'Moreover the crystal says that, In the year 1906 thy likeness shall be placed upon a picture postcard!'" He forgot to mention that the card would be highly collectible and worth over $25 today!

Seers are most often asked questions about matters of love. Artist A. Taylor, series K177. $10.

A. Boito, music sheet for *Mephistopheles*, printed in Italy for the French market, pre-1900. $40.

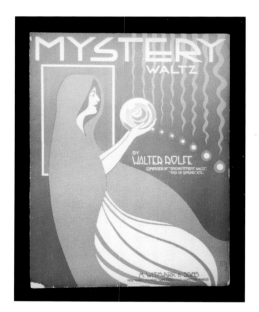

Mystery Waltz by Walter Rolfe. $30.

A quality crystal ball with provenience like this one is rare indeed. It is flawless, highly sensitive, historic, and a joy to be allowed to use. This ball came from Lexington, Kentucky, and is from the house of the famous madam, Bell Breezing (a.k.a... Watling from *Gone With The Wind*). It was used for parlor games and to amuse "the Gentlemen" visitors. $3500.

A 1940s humor card. I wonder if this seer is still doing gigs at parties in the Harvard, New York, area! $4.

This is a marvelous little children's booklet given away by Loose-Wiles Biscuit Co. (revised 1924, 3rd edition). Using the crystal, the children are taken to different countries. $35.

This small crystal ball, because of the stand, probably dates from the 1920s. Of good quality, it is clear and an excellent focus. $125.

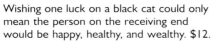

Harrison Fisher was one of the great illustrators and molders of womens' mystic beauty. Here is one of the Fisher Girls at her most mysterious and demure. Reinthal & Newman, #847. $25.

Wishing one luck on a black cat could only mean the person on the receiving end would be happy, healthy, and wealthy. $12.

Italian artcard, Il Futuro series, 1020-6. $35.

A happy medium is one who gives a good fortune and gets paid well for it! $4.

"Owl," with a game on the reverse. $35.

Fortune Feathers, A Halloween Party Game, designed by Peggy Geistel. Pin the fortune on the owl. $15.

Luhrs made this Crystal Fortunes Game, with a moving wheel that shows the number in the crystal ball. Depending on your gender, you would read the corresponding fortune below. $40.

Crystal Fortunes, made in USA by Luhrs. $45.

Old Witch Brewsome Stunts. $15.

Jack O' Lantern Fortune Game by Beistle Co. $55.

Zingo Halloween Fortune and Stunt Game, 1935, by the Beistle Co. $45.

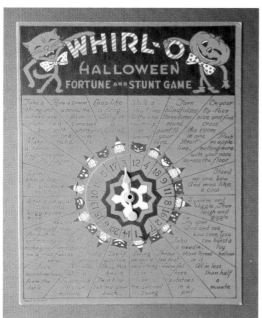

Whirl-O Fortune and Stunt Game by Beistle Co. $30.

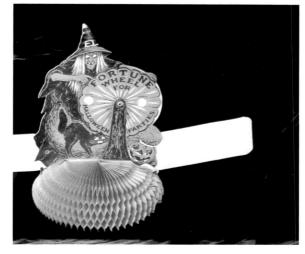

A fortune wheel centerpiece game. The honeycomb bottom makes it decorative. The two tabs can be pulled down, with fortunes to be read, when game time begins. $50.

H.E. Luhrs Stunt Halloween Quiz. $35.

Label from Phrenological Character Game by Milton Bradley & Co. $20.

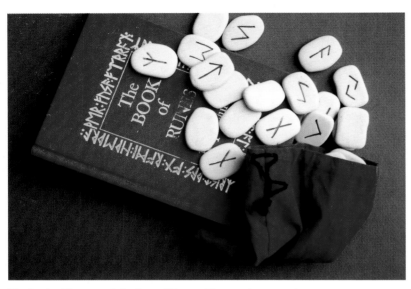

These are Zodiac games. The one in plastic is worth $8. The cut crystal belonged to Gerald Gardner, who had the Witch Museum on the Isle of Mann. $100.

The Book of Runes and the bag of Runes. This can be turned into a group game by letting each person choose one and then reading the fortune of the person. It is better than fortune cookies, unless you wrote the fortunes yourself! $45.

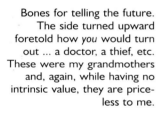

Bones for telling the future. The side turned upward foretold how *you* would turn out ... a doctor, a thief, etc. These were my grandmothers and, again, while having no intrinsic value, they are priceless to me.

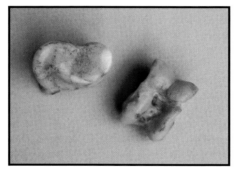

These are among my prized possessions. They are beans my grandmother told fortunes with. Though I play with them quite often, I still haven't learned the meaning of the separations or how she could be so accurate about so many things. Value? Priceless to me.

Left and far left: The original program and postcard from Noel Coward's play, *Blithe Spirit*. This play has to be one of the most revived shows of all times. Seances are fun all year long, not just on Halloween, and nobody is wittier and funnier than Coward. If you haven't seen the movie or the play, do so. It is ever fresh. Postcard, $20; program, $40.

Royal Doulton figurine. *From the collection of Thomas Godard of the Haunted Mansion.* $150.

Reading palms is a grand pastime at parties. Place your hand in this Plexiglas stand and everyone may read of your shortcomings ... among other things! $55.

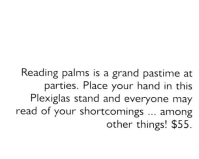

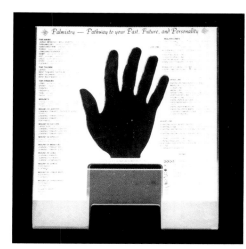

Jewish humor postcard. The crystal ball can be the source of humor. $30.

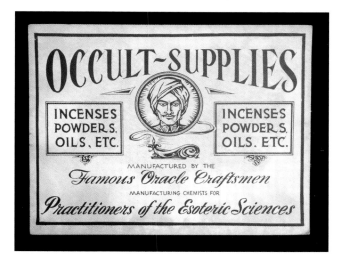

Occult-Supplies sign. Well, perhaps this doesn't belong in this section, but if you will play at the esoteric sciences, it is always fun to set the mood. "You will marry a man who likes to cook, a baker he will be." Burn some cinnamon incense at this point in a party and then ask everyone if they would like some apple pie! Sign, $75—with or without the pie!

Witch of Endor boxed spin game. $95.

Le Miraculeux. Fortune telling games are international in appeal. $75.

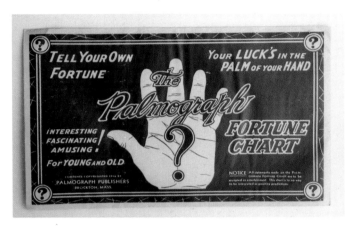

The Palmograph Fortune Chart, in original packaging, ca. 1936. $50.

Palm Reading key chain. *Modern gift from Rebecca Venable*. $12.

Below
I'm a Dumbskull is a stunt forfeit-type game. Spinner card has stunts to be performed on the reverse. Original envelope, $65.

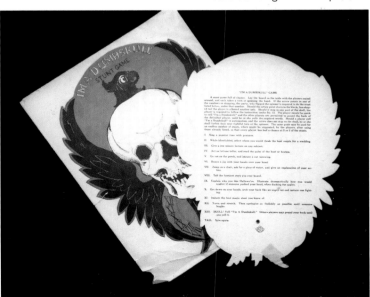

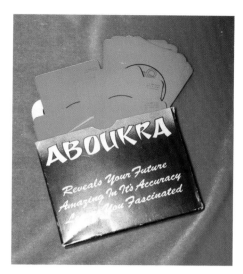

Aboukra fortune telling deck. $15.

Fortune Telling Crystal Ball, with
original box. $45.

Dickinson's Witch Hazel Puzzle, front and back. $45.

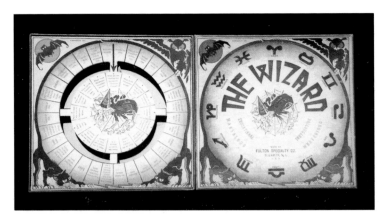

The Wizard, boxed game by Fulton. $45.

Front and back views of the Ghostly Stunt and Fortune Game. $25.

This is a greeting card; however, it is also one of those infuriating games that some do too quickly while others can't quite get all the little metal balls into the holes at one time! $8.